THE CHRISTIAN USE
OF EMOTIONAL POWER

THE CHRISTIAN USE OF EMOTIONAL POWER

H. NORMAN WRIGHT

Fleming H. Revell Company
Old Tappan, New Jersey

Excerpt from BORN AFTER MIDNIGHT by A. W. Tozer is used by permission of Christian Publications, Inc., Harrisburg, Pennsylvania 17101.

Excerpts from THE PURSUIT OF HAPPINESS by Spiros Zodhiates, published by William B. Eerdmans, are reprinted by permission of Rev. Zodhiates.

Excerpt from newspaper article is from "Anger—Sorrow Can Cost Your Life" and used by permission of Independent, Press-Telegram, P.O. Box 230, Long Beach, California 90844.

Excerpts from DEPRESSION:CAUSES AND TREATMENT by Aaron T. Beck M.D., published by University of Pennsylvania Press, are used by permission of Dr. Beck.

Excerpt from ME, MYSELF AND YOU by Vincent Collins is used by permission of Abbey Press.

Excerpt from WINGED LIFE by Hannah Hurnard is used by permission of Artype Services, Portland, Oregon.

Excerpt from CYCLE OF VICTORIOUS LIVING by Earl G. Lee is used by permission of Beacon Hill Press of Kansas City.

Excerpts from THE CHRISTIAN'S HANDBOOK OF PSYCHIATRY by O. Quentin Hyder M.D., Copyrighted © 1971 by Fleming H. Revell Company are used by permission.

Excerpt from THE ART OF UNDERSTANDING YOURSELF by Cecil Osborne is used by permission of Zondervan Publishing House.

Excerpt from THE DYNAMICS OF PERSONAL ADJUSTMENT by George F. J. Lehner and Ella Kube, Second Edition © 1964 is reprinted by permission of Prentice-Hall, Inc., Englewood Cliffs, New Jersey.

Excerpt from PEACE OF MIND by Joshua Liebman is used by permission of Simon and Schuster.

Excerpts from CREATIVE AND CRITICAL THINKING by W. Edgar Moore, Copyright © Houghton Mifflin Company, 1967 are used by permission.

Excerpt from ANSWER TO ANXIETY by Herman W. Gockel, copyright 1961 by Concordia Publishing House is used by permission.

Excerpts reprinted from CARING ENOUGH TO CONFRONT (a Regal Book) by David Augsburger are by permission of G/L Publications, Glendale, California 91209. © Copyright 1974 under the title, THE LOVE FIGHT, by Herald Press, Scottdale, Pa. 15683.

Excerpt by John Powell is from WHY AM I AFRAID TO TELL YOU WHO I AM? Reprinted with permission of Argus Communications, Niles, Illinois 60648.

Library of Congress Cataloging in Publication Data

Wright, H Norman.
    The Christian use of emotional power.

    Bibliography: p.
    1. Emotions.   2.   Christian life—1960–
I. Title.
BF561.W74   248'.4   74–10755
ISBN 0-8007-0679-X

TO those who have enriched my life so much—
my mother and father, my wife Joycelin and my
children, Sheryl and Matthew

Contents

1
Emotions—Where Do They Come From?

The steam of behavior is only visible proof that the fire of thought is boiling the water of emotion. A heavy lid may curb the steam of action but unless we curb the fire of thinking the heaviest lid possible will blow and high will be the blast of it. Obviously, therefore, we lose spiritual battles not by failing to restrain our actions with heavier lids, we are defeated because we do not change our flaming thoughts that boil the waters of emotion.

LOREN FISCHER
Highway to Dynamic Living

Have you ever tried to fall asleep when you were excited or upset? Instead of drifting peacefully off to sleep, you no doubt found your mind racing a hundred miles an hour as you tossed and turned until all hours of the early morning. Have you ever waited outside an office for an interview with your heart pounding wildly, perspiration on your brow, and your mouth bone-dry? Or have you ever spent hours preparing for an exam, only to find that when the exam was placed on your desk, you couldn't remember a thing? Have you ever become so upset or angry with another person that you couldn't think what to say?

All of us experience strong emotional feelings because we were all created as emotional beings. Some of the emotions we feel are love, tenderness, anger, rage, disgust, fear, terror, sympathy, elation, depression, and jealousy. The Scriptures describe many of these emotional reactions.

As grieved *and* mourning, yet [we are] always rejoicing; as poor [ourselves, yet] bestowing riches on many; as having nothing, and [yet in reality] possessing all things.

2 Corinthians 6:10 AMPLIFIED

For God did not give us a spirit of timidity—of cowardice, of craven and cringing and fawning fear—but [He has given us a spirit] of power and of love and of calm *and* well-balanced mind *and* discipline *and* self-control.

2 Timothy 1:7 AMPLIFIED

When angry, do not sin; do not ever let your wrath—your exasperation, your fury or indignation—last until the sun goes down.

Ephesians 4:26 AMPLIFIED

I heard, and my [whole inner self] trembled, my lips quivered at the sound. Rottenness enters into my bones and under me—down *to my feet*—I tremble. I will wait quietly for the day of trouble and distress, when there shall come up against [my] people him who is about to invade *and* oppress them.

Habakkuk 3:16 AMPLIFIED

And Abel brought of the first-born of his flock and of the fat portions. And the Lord had respect *and* regard for Abel and for his offering. But for Cain and his offering He had no respect *or* regard. So Cain was exceedingly angry *and* indignant, and he looked sad *and* depressed.

Genesis 4:4,5 AMPLIFIED

And Jacob served seven years for Rachel; and they seemed to him but a few days, because of the love he had for her.

Genesis 29:20 AMPLIFIED

[Share others' joy], rejoicing with those who rejoice; and [share others' grief], weeping with those who weep.

Romans 12:15 AMPLIFIED

Emotions are a mixed blessing. They are responsible for many of man's finest and greatest achievements. They are also responsible for some of the greatest tragedies in our world.

We usually talk about emotions in terms of how we *feel.* I *feel* angry. I *feel* disgusted. I *feel* depressed. Although the words *emotion* and *feeling* are often used interchangeably, there *are* differences between them. Perhaps we could define *feeling* as experiences of mild intensity, and *emotion* as those which move us strongly.

Emotions may arise from either external or internal stimulation—a condition in the body or a thought in the mind. Technically, emotion may be defined as: an acute disturbance or upset of the individual which is revealed in behavior and in conscious experience as well as through widespread changes in the functioning of viscera (smooth muscles, glands, heart and lungs) and which is initiated by factors within a psychological situation.

Several elements are involved in an emotion. It is usually sudden in onset, temporary, and disrupts, disturbs or disorganizes the total person. An emotional reaction to a stimulus involves both past reactions to a similar stimulus and the individual's present psychological condition. It also involves behavior, for we usually observe certain types of behavior in an emotional reaction. Because the intellect is involved in emotional experiences, conscious experience is present. The physical part of the body is also involved because of the various organs which are affected.

Emotions produce chemical and neurological changes within the body. They produce energy which mobilizes a person and keeps him alive and functioning. When you experience fear, energy becomes available which helps you run away from danger. Anger can provide you with the energy you need to survive by fighting for your life. The maternal feelings of a mother provide the love that infants need to survive.

Emotions are similar to reflex action. In a given situation you will feel a particular emotion. If you touch the cornea of your eye with a handkerchief your eyelid will blink. There is no way you can stop that reflex from happening. When the eye is touched, certain nerve cells are activated and a message is sent to your brain. Other nerves are put into action until the message arrives back at the eye and the eyelid blinks. Once the cornea is touched, the eyelid blinks automatically.

Our emotions are quite similar. If you stub your toe your immediate reaction is to get upset or angry. You may say to yourself, "I won't get upset! I won't get mad! I won't!" But if your toe hurts badly enough you will still get upset. You cannot prevent the emotion, but you can control what you do with that emotion.

Sometimes we experience a strong emotion and are not aware of it. Fear may manifest itself as tenseness.

Anger might manifest itself as hurt feelings, depression, fear, or insomnia. At other times we may be afraid or angry and not know why we feel that way. Each day we experience stimuli that trigger emotional reactions. It is even possible for the memory of a past event to arouse an emotion. When this emotional energy is aroused it must be directed into the proper outlet. If it is not, it does not disappear. If anything, it will increase until it overflows. Emotions that are not expressed through healthy outlets such as play, work, and talking about our feelings, usually end up directed toward certain organs of the body. (This will be discussed in greater detail in later chapters.)

Emotions are aroused when a person makes a value judgment. This judgment is usually made on the basis of sensory appeal or repulsion and rational evaluation. For example, something you like may provide you with great pleasure and satisfaction but, from a rational standpoint, it might be bad for you. A chocolate candy bar may be very desirable to the diabetic but if he eats it he knows he will suffer the consequences. A college student may want to skip his classes and go to the beach, but if he gives in to that desire he may flunk his examinations.

If it were possible to look into a person's mind we would find a process occurring of which the person may not even be aware. An emotional reaction is preceded by knowledge, evaluation, and finally, judgment. But these occur so rapidly and even unconsciously that you might not be aware of them happening at all. After the judgment has been made the emotional reaction follows with the appropriate muscular and glandular changes which are a part of emotional activity.

Emotions involve reactions and experiences which

come about as we adjust to life situations. They are tied to intellectual functions because a person first has to perceive and understand something about a situation before his emotions come into play.

The meaning of any situation is gradually built up during a person's lifetime because of innumerable experiences with similar situations. If a person has five bad experiences with dogs, one after another, naturally a fear response is gradually reinforced.

Why do some people react differently than others? Are they *more emotional* or are some people *less emotional?* Is there a normal way people should react? Each person reacts emotionally because of the influences and experiences of his own childhood and background. Some individuals feel great intensities of emotions and react with intense joy or disappointment. And then we run into the person who seems to be insulated from such depth of feeling.

Differences of emotional expression can sometimes be attributed to constitutional makeup. Some babies almost immediately are more excitable than others. Their nervous systems seem to be more sensitive. Early training also plays a part. Some children are taught to deny and hide their emotions, others are encouraged to express them. Transient factors such as fatigue, illness, and alcohol can affect emotional response. Brain damage will also cause variations.

Still another factor is a person's frame of reference. The feelings a person has and the way he expresses and controls them depend on his basic beliefs and attitudes about what is true, right, and possible. He actually reacts to a situation according to his own needs.

Finally, a person's cultural background and environment will affect his emotional reaction. If you live in a highly competitive, hostile society you will probably reflect that with a lack of love and sympathy.

The intensity of an emotion depends not only on how attractive or repulsive or dangerous we judge a situation to be, but also on how important this attraction is for us and how much we would mind having to put up with the negative features. We *can* order and regulate the intensity of an emotion if we consider the emotional situation in its relation to the goal we determined. This can result in a significant reduction in the degree of its appeal or repulsion.

There is a balance wherein two different people can react differently and still be considered normal. Outside of that norm, however, emotional reactions can be considered out of balance. A very superficial reaction may indicate a protective type of rigid life-style.

While we usually are not able to control an emotional response to a particular stimulus, we *can* control how we will express that emotion. If you feel hate, you do not have to act hateful. When you stub your toe you can choose how you will react. You can kick whatever you hit, say "ouch," swear, or hop about on one foot. If you walk into a strange yard and a mountain lion starts coming toward you, you will naturally feel fear. You can choose to run, climb a tree, yell for help, or pick up a stick and run toward the animal. But you will still be afraid initially.

If you always react a particular way to certain stimuli, you may feel it is impossible to react differently. Even if you do react out of a habit pattern, you can choose to react differently and try a new pattern. If the channels of a dam are opened, allowing the water to flow out, nothing will hold back that water. But the water can be controlled and diverted into different stream beds. In similar fashion you can divert your emotional energy into healthy and useful channels.

2
The Control of Our Emotions

Search me [thoroughly], O God, and know my heart! Try me and know my thoughts! And see if there is any wicked or hurtful way in me, and lead me in the way everlasting.

Psalms 139: 23, 24 AMPLIFIED

Emotional development begins at birth, perhaps even prior to birth. As the image we have of ourselves begins to form we learn how to trust or not to trust. We experience fear, jealousy, anger, sadness, joy, elation, happiness, and other emotional reactions. Our emotions grow and develop in different ways. One person may develop a balanced emotional life, another an imbalance. For some, emotional control is easier than for others.

Our emotions play a large part in making our lives meaningful or miserable. C. B. Eavey, in his book *Principles of Mental Health for Christian Living* suggests:

Nothing in us so defiles and destroys the beauty and the glory of living as do emotions; nothing so elevates, purifies, enriches, and strengthens life as does emotion. Through our emotions we can have the worst or the best, we can descend to the lowest depths, or we can rise to the highest heights. Every normal human being has a longing for the overflowing of natural emotion. Without capacity to experience emotions suitable to the situations we meet, we would not be normal. Emotions of the right kind, expressed in the proper way, make life beautiful, full, and rich, rob it of monotony, and contribute much to both the enjoyment and the effectiveness of living.

Our emotions are a gift from God for we were created as emotional beings. Because of the fall, man's emotional life often becomes distorted. But our emotions as such should never be despised, expelled, ignored, or even neglected. "If we try to drive out any one of them," adds Eavey, "we simply intensify its activity. When we let them go without guidance and control, they cause confusion and riot in our lives. If we try to suppress them, they produce destruction in our personalities."

For better or for worse, our emotions are an important part of us. Whether they are *better* or *worse* depends upon our use of them.

There are four processes which are indispensable to the way we express our emotions. First we *perceive or sense* something, such as seeing, tasting, smelling, or feeling. Second, we *act*—walking, eating, climbing, and so on. Third, we *feel*, as in love, fear, hate, depression. Finally, we *reason or think*, such as imagining, making hypotheses, solving problems, and making conclusions. Some people place the emphasis more upon one than the other. Some people perceive, act, *think*, and feel. The more emotional person, however, perceives, acts, thinks, and *feels.* All people think and feel but the different ways in which we think affects how we feel.

For example, here is a young lady who is very dejected and upset. When asked why, she says it is because her boyfriend has rejected her. What she is actually saying is that the rejection is causing the depression. However, that is not entirely true. Her subjective interpretation of the rejection is the real cause. "It is awful to be rejected like that," she thinks. "I am deeply hurt. Why did this happen to me? It shouldn't happen to me. I must be a failure. I am also unattractive. There must be something wrong with me." Messages and thoughts like these are the factors bringing on the depression. Statements like, "It shouldn't happen to me. I must be a failure. I am unattractive," are neither rational nor true. Why *shouldn't* this happen? No one is immune to rejection at some time in his life. Just because it happened does not mean that the person is unattractive or a failure! Irrational messages such as these bring about the emotional reaction of depression. It is normal for a person to be upset and sad when a relationship is broken but not to that extent. It would be better for this girl to think rationally, "I am sad because of this situation and I wish it could have worked out. I will miss him. This is unfortunate but it is not the end of the world." In most cases it is not the event or circumstance that brings about an emotional reaction but our interpretation of it.

Mild emotions have a tonic effect upon the mind, increasing mental alertness and endurance. A small amount of concern or fear, for example, can make a person more alert for study or performance. At the same time, however, these mild emotions can hamper our thinking and objectivity, for when we are threatened, what is the natural thing to do? We defend ourselves, choosing self-defensive behavior.

Strong emotions affect our thinking even more. *Strong emotions can interfere with our learning.* If a student is overly fearful of failure in school he may find himself studying without grasping the meaning of what he is reading.

A strong emotion tends to inhibit the ability to recall what a person has learned. Take, for example, the individual who studies hard for an exam and really learns the material, but is unable to remember any of the material during the examination because of his intense fear of failure. This individual actually brings about the very thing he is afraid will happen.

Strong emotion narrows perception. When you are very angry you tend to perceive only the elements in the situation that enhance your anger. Your child has been a pest most of the day and you become angry. What you probably see and remember about your child at that moment is only the bad behavior. You overlook the several occasions on this day when your child was helpful and cooperative. The same reaction occurs with fear—you tend to focus on those elements which feed your fear.

During times like these your creative and critical thinking is limited. You are apt to make generalizations and exaggerations. You're angry at your wife and you begin to make accusations. "You're never on time. You're always late and making me be late. No one could be as slow as you." Then you may extend this generalization to her relatives. "You learned to be late because of those slowpokes in your family. I've also noticed that the friends you pick are duds too!" And the generalizations continue!

When a person overreacts emotionally he *spends his time thinking about the threat or problem instead of the solution.* A person who has to give an important speech begins to be fearful over making mistakes and creating a bad impression. Now this *is* a possibility. But because of his overconcern with it happening it is even more likely to occur. It would be much better for him to direct this energy toward learning and practicing the speech. In place of visualizing oneself failing when giving a speech, why not visualize making a successful presentation? Why not go over in one's mind the specific steps necessary to bring about that success?

Strong emotions also tend to reduce the control of behavior by thought. When you have a strong emotion you feel an urge to do something immediately instead of waiting to consider it in the light of accumulated experience. This is the problem of acting first and thinking later. This type of impulsive behavior can bring on greater difficulties.

Several scriptural passages caution against acting first and thinking later. Some of these have to do with speech and our emotions.

> Understand [this] my beloved brethren. Let every man be quick to hear, (a ready listener,) slow to speak, slow to take offense *and* to get angry.
>
> James 1:19 AMPLIFIED

> A hot-tempered man stirs up strife, but he who is slow to anger appeases contention.
>
> Proverbs 15:18 AMPLIFIED

> He who is slow to anger is better than the mighty, and he who rules his *own* spirit than he who takes a city.
>
> Proverbs 16:32 AMPLIFIED

The earlier we begin to think in opposition to the emotion the easier it is to go counter to that emotion. The messages you send yourself in your mind are the determining factor in what is done with that feeling or emotion. All of this takes effort and energy, for it is going counter to the actual effort of emotions upon our thinking ability.

One of the greatest hindrances to emotional control is the mind-set. This means that a person views a situation in a preset manner, regardless of the evidence. It is like a person saying, "Don't bother me with the facts, my mind is made up." A person whose mind is set perceives what he expects to perceive. You are certain that someone at a social gathering is going to reject you or avoid you and because of this certainty in your mind you begin looking for this rejection. You may even interpret a neutral comment as a rejection. Dogmatism, lack of objectivity, pushing ahead with blinders on seem to be characteristics of people with a mind-set. In *Creative and Critical Thinking*, W. Edgar Moore writes:

The damage a mind-set can do is dramatically illustrated by the sinking of the *Titanic* on her maiden voyage in 1912, with the loss of 1,513 lives. Designed to be the safest ship afloat, the *Titanic* was equipped with a double bottom and sixteen watertight compartments. A mind-set that she was unsinkable seems to have been largely responsible for the disaster.

She carried lifeboats sufficient for only one-third of her capacity, and no assignment of passengers was made to these boats; nor were any drills held. The *Titanic* was unsinkable.

Three days out of Queenstown, she received her first wireless warning of icebergs in the steamer lanes. A few hours later she received another message about icebergs, but the wireless operator was too busy with his accounts to bother recording the message. The *Titanic* was unsinkable.

That afternoon another warning was received. This time the operator sent it to the Captain, who glanced at it casually and handed it without comment to the managing director of the White Star Line. By 9:30 that night at least five warnings of icebergs had been received, and the *Titanic* was nearing their reported location. But no precautions were taken other than to warn the lookouts to be alert. The owners wanted a speed record; the *Titanic* steamed ahead into the darkness at twenty-two knots. The *Titanic* was unsinkable.

She had yet another chance. At 11:30 P.M. the wireless crackled with a message from the *Californian:* "Say, old man, we are stuck here, surrounded by ice." But the mindset held, and the *Titanic's* operator replied, "Shut up, shut up, keep out. I am talking to Cape Race; you are jamming my signals." The *Titanic* steamed ahead at twenty-two knots; she was unsinkable.

Ten minutes later the lookout spotted a giant iceberg dead ahead. Officers on the bridge did what they could to avoid the crash, but it was too late. The collision ripped a hundred-yard gash in the ship's double bottom. Although the water-tight doors were closed immediately, the bulkheads not already damaged gave way, one by one. The great ship was doomed.

The loading of the lifeboats went slowly and badly, in part because the passengers would not believe that so safe a ship could sink. The boats left the ship with nearly five hundred passengers less than capacity. At best there would have been room for no more than a thousand. Even so the casualties might have been few. Distress calls were sent out within minutes after the collision, and the ship did not sink until more than two hours later. A number of ships raced to the scene, in spite of the ice. But they were too far away to save the fifteen hundred who did not get into the lifeboats. Meantime, the *Californian* was lying within sight of the *Titanic,* possibly no more than five miles away. Her radio operator did not hear the *Titanic*'s wireless calls; he had gone to bed shortly after being told to "shut up." Some of her crew did see the *Titanic*'s lights and rocket signals but did nothing more than try to communicate with the unknown ship by blinker. Testimony in the investigation of the disaster showed that the sea was calm and the night clear, and that the *Californian* might easily have pushed through the ice field to rescue most if not all of the passengers. Perhaps her officers, too, had a mind-set.

A second hindrance to emotional control is the way we interpret situations or events. "A man is hurt not so much by what happens," wrote Montaigne the essayist, "as by his opinion of what happens." In *The Encheiridion* Epictetus observed that, "Men are disturbed not by things, but by the views which they take of them." Shakespeare rephrased this in *Hamlet:* "There is nothing either good or bad, but thinking makes it so." Collins, in *Me, Myself and You* suggested, "It is not our situation that makes us happy or miserable, it's the way in which we react to it."

The basis for emotional control is in your interpretation of any situation. People react to situations not always as they are but as they interpret them. Two people can have totally different reactions because of their background and experience. Encountering a snake in a field may elicit fear in a person unaccustomed to them, while a snake handler will have no fear at all.

When a person finds himself reacting emotionally he can begin to reinterpret or rethink what is happening. For example, Moore illustrates in *Creative and Critical Thinking:*

Suppose you find yourself in this situation. When you entered college, your parents brought you to the campus, selected your room and your roommates, told you what courses to study, paid your fees for the semester, gave you twenty-five dollars for pocket money, and instructed you to write for more when needed. Your grades for the first semester were low. Now, at the beginning of the second semester, your parents hand you a check for your expenses for the semester, tell you that you will receive no more, let you get back to the campus by yourself, show no interest in what courses you will take or where you room, and make no comment about your low grades.

You might, as many students would, conclude that your parents are angry because you made low grades. But these facts could be explained by three other hypotheses: (1) your parents are too occupied with other matters to give you their usual attention; (2) they are disappointed with your grades and believe you will do better if left on your own; (3) your parents now have enough confidence in you to let you manage your own life. The habit of setting up rival hypotheses is a good one to cultivate, especially in interpreting personal matters. You will often discover that you have interpreted a situation inaccurately, and that your fear or anger was not justified.

Another example of this type of thinking can be seen in the woman whose pastor always greets her after the church service on Sunday. But as she was leaving on one particular Sunday the pastor did not say anything to her. He did not even acknowledge that she was there. The woman became upset and by the time she arrived home she was *very* upset. The reason could be traced to the message she was sending herself. In her mind she was saying, "The pastor must be upset with me. Perhaps he is mad at me. He was very rude. He should have spoken to me or at least smiled at me. I wonder if he thinks I have done something wrong or sinned. Maybe he is tired of having to speak to me each Sunday and he would rather talk to others."

This type of thinking will obviously disturb a person. A better way would be for the woman to consider the alternatives. Instead of assuming the pastor is displeased with her she might think, "I wonder why the pastor was so preoccupied today. He didn't have a chance to speak to me. He must have a lot on his mind or be tired. There were many new visitors today, too, and he needed to speak to them. I guess I can feel fortunate that he has taken so much time in the past with me. It isn't everyone who has that opportunity. I will certainly continue to remember him in prayer, with all that he has to do." This thinking is constructive for both parties and brings on feelings of love and compassion instead of rejection.

All of us experience times in our lives when things do not go as we have planned. Perhaps in some way we are partly responsible for situations not working out as they should. But getting extremely upset over a given set of circumstances will rarely help to change them for the better. Actually the more upset a person becomes over the unpleasant situations of life, the more disorganized and ineffective will be his efforts to improve the existing conditions.

Feelings such as fear and anger can be useful if they are controlled, but when they are not controlled they become destructive. Feelings of failure, inadequacy, self-pity, depression, and guilt also disrupt a person's emotional balance. With the help of the Holy Spirit, all of these can be brought under control.

How then can we learn to control our emotions? The first step toward achieving emotional balance is the *new birth.*

> For God so loved the world, that He gave His only begotten Son, that whoever believes in Him should not perish, but have eternal life.
>
> John 3:16 NAS

> He who believes in the Son has eternal life.
>
> John 3:36 NAS

> And the witness is this, that God has given us eternal life, and this life is in His Son. He who has the Son has the life; he who does not have the Son of God does not have the life.
>
> 1 John 5:11, 12 NAS

A non-Christian can experience emotional balance to a limited degree and appear quite well adjusted. A Christian, however, has the *potential* and *means* available for complete emotional balance.

Some people think that once a person accepts Jesus Christ as his Saviour, emotional balance comes about immediately and automatically. It does neither! An emotionally stable person will have more to build upon initially in his Christian life than the unstable. The emotionally damaged person and the emotional infant do not become emotionally mature or healed by regeneration. Growth in the Christian life is a process and part of that process is emotional growth. It is not the fault of Christianity or the teachings of Scripture if a Christian does not achieve this control. *But for those who are willing to turn their emotions over to God, control is possible.*

The goal of our emotional development is found in the emotions or attitudes expressed in the Fruit of the Spirit in Galatians 5:22, 23 NAS. *But the fruit of the Spirit is love, joy, peace, patience, kindness, goodness, faithfulness, gentleness, self-control; against such things there is no law.* Here we find the healing emotions of life such as faith, hope, joy, peace, self-control, and love.

The second vital step towards emotional balance is to learn to react properly to our emotions. The worst possible manner of dealing with our emotions is to deny or ignore them. Our bodies are structured to respond automatically to emotional stimulation. The energy that is generated when we feel an emotion must find a healthy outlet. If it does not, it will find expression in some unnatural manner.

Repression and denial simply do not work. Actually emotional turmoil has the potential for being more beneficial than complete loss of feeling. It is easy to envy the person who seems to have everything under control, who appears incapable of grief or anger. However, his so-called stability may be a too rigid emotional insulation and lack of feeling, a brittle rigidity that may eventually snap.

A person should never lose touch with his feelings. Facing, recognizing, and dealing with the emotion and its cause is healthy. This does not mean we should be constantly taking our emotional temperature. It simply means we should honestly recognize and accept what we are like.

Once you have faced your emotions squarely there are three different ways to control them. Severely disturbed people may need to have their emotions influenced directly through electrical or biochemical means—shock treatment, barbiturates or tranquilizers. A second means is through relaxation exercises or breathing techniques. For most people, however, *it is possible to control your feelings by controlling your thoughts (and at times your behavior)*. We call this the willing-thinking process.

Emotions usually arise because of our thought patterns. An outside stimulus may trigger the emotion and then we allow the emotion to dominate our thinking. We cannot stop the stimulus nor our immediate reaction to it, but we do have something to say about the intensity and duration of it. This is where imagination comes into play. Vincent Collins in *Me, Myself and You* suggests:

The reaction process is further complicated by that faculty of the mind which we call "Imagination." Imagination is to the emotions what illustrations are to a text, what music is to a ballad. It is the ability to form mental pictures, to visualize irritating or fearful situations in concrete form. As soon as we perceive a feeling and begin to think about it, the imagination goes to work. The imagination reinforces the thoughts, the thoughts intensify the feelings, and the whole business builds up. There is only one way to beat this game, and that is to *stop the thoughts in their tracks* and block out the imaginary pictures. Fearful or angry feelings and thoughts generate pressure, and the pressure will continue to increase as long as the build-up process is allowed to continue.

In *Winged Life* Hannah Hurnard writes:

Alexander Whyte has rightly and wonderfully described this greatest of all gifts which God has given us. He says of the imagination: "It makes us full of eyes, without and within." The imagination is far stronger than any other power which we possess, and the psychologists tell us that on occasions, when the will and the imagination are in conflict, the imagination always wins. How important therefore that we should vow by the Saviour's help never to throw the wrong kind of pictures on this screen in our minds, for the imagination literally has the power of making the things we picture real and effective.

We may not always be able to prevent the wrong pictures from flashing on the screen, but we don't need to indulge ourselves in the images. As Hurnard explains, "Every worrier and every person tormented with fear, knows this only too well. Never picture anything you are afraid of, or the fear will become more real than reality itself."

Thus we see in Scripture (*italics* added):

And God saw that the wickedness of man was great in the earth and that *every imagination of the thoughts of his heart* was only evil continually.

Genesis 6:5 KJV

And thou, Solomon my son, know thou the God of thy father, and serve him with a perfect heart and with a willing mind: for the Lord searcheth all hearts, and understandeth *all the imaginations of the thoughts:* if thou seek him, he will be found of thee; but if thou forsake him, he will cast thee off for ever.

1 Chronicles 28:9 KJV

Evil imagination led to man becoming corrupt in those days, and the same process is at work today. The last war was largely brought about by the evil imagination of Adolf Hitler, who wrote down his thoughts in *Mein Kampf* years before he carried them into action.

People who are worriers find that their imagination is usually the root cause of their trouble. Imagination does not have to be negative. It is a gift from God and the mother of ambition and creativity. A beautiful picture or a great cathedral once existed only in the minds of the artists who designed them. As Isaiah said, *He will keep you in perfect peace whose mind (imagination) is stayed on Thee (see Isaiah 26:3 AMPLIFIED).*

A large part of what people call emotion is nothing more nor less than biased or strongly evaluative thinking. A person who tends to react emotionally uses only part of the information available to him. A thinking person is less strongly biased by his previous experience and controls his imagination.

With practice you can learn to turn your thoughts off and on. To do so you must put things into their proper perspective. Some people argue that, "When I experience an emotion there's no stopping it. It just goes on and I act upon it." Certainly the emotion will not be stopped or eliminated completely and immediately. But its intensity can be controlled and eventually the reaction eliminated. The more a person practices control the greater the possibility of immediate control. *We do not have to act in accordance with our emotion.*

If you are afraid of something you probably run away from whatever it is you fear. This may be actual flight or just staying where you are so you won't contact the feared object. Acting counter to this emotion is difficult, but possible. For example, you may decide that swimming in a certain river is not safe because of the current and temperature of the water. You may feel fear every

time you think about it or when you get too close to the
river. But suppose your son suddenly becomes ill and
the help he needs is on the other side of the river. The
only way to get to the other side is to swim. You will
decide to swim in spite of your fear of the water. Control is possible when we make reasonable decisions in
our minds.

If you feel frustrated because you are being deprived
of something, you need to ask yourself, "Is it a dire
necessity that I have this or accomplish this? Why is it
so important to me? Is it what I think is best for me?
Have I considered whether God would feel this is best
for me?" If the situation is extremely unpleasant, face
the situation with calmness and work at improving the
conditions. If, for now, the situation cannot be changed,
accept it and go on. Make the most of frustrating situations by accepting them as challenges. Instead of giving
in to frustration, say to yourself, "It's too bad about this
situation. I'm frustrated but it certainly won't kill me.
I can learn to live in this situation and make the best of
it. I would like it to be different but I will take it a step
at a time." Ask God what He wants to teach us through
the situation.

A certain young man and his older sister came from
a family which had a high incidence of diabetes. Neither of them had the disease but they were both aware
of the strong possibility that they might some day contract it. The sister became emotionally disturbed over
the situation simply by the messages she kept sending
herself. She was extremely fearful and worried. Her
thoughts went something like this: "Wouldn't it be terrible if I had that dread disease? What would I do? What
would happen to me? Would others like me? Would
they want me around them?" The young man, on the

other hand, took the attitude, "It would be a nuisance if I became a diabetic. It would cause some adjustment but it would not be terrible. I could learn to live with it as so many others have done."

> All the days of the desponding afflicted are made evil [by anxious thoughts and foreboding], but he who has a glad heart has a continual feast [regardless of circumstances].
>
> Proverbs 15:15 AMPLIFIED

The Apostle Paul said:

> Not that I am implying that I was in any personal want, for I have learned how to be content (satisfied to the point where I am not disturbed or disquieted) in whatever state I am. I know how to be abased *and* live humbly in straitened circumstances, and I know also how to enjoy plenty *and* live in abundance. I have learned in any and all circumstances, the secret of facing every situation, whether well-fed or going hungry, having a sufficiency *and* to spare or going without *and* being in want.
>
> Philippians 4:11, 12 AMPLIFIED

When Paul wrote this he was in prison, probably chained to a soldier! But he indicates by the word *content* that he is self-sufficient, independent of circumstances, conditions or surroundings. In *Spiritual Depression* Martyn Lloyd-Jones explains:

> To put it positively, . . . what the apostle says here is that he is not mastered or controlled by circumstances. By all means if you can improve your circumstances by fair and

legitimate means, do so; but if you cannot, and if you have to remain in a trying and difficult position, do not be mastered by it, do not let it get you down, do not let it control you, do not let it determine your misery or your joy.

3
Controlling Your Thoughts

The thoughts I think, the words I speak, the actions
I take, the emotions I feel—they are mine, for them
I am fully responsible.

DAVID W. AUGSBURGER
Caring Enough to Confront

The Scriptures have much to say about thinking and
the thought-life. The words *think, thought,* and *mind*
are used over three hundred times in the Bible. The
Book of Proverbs says, *As a man thinketh in his heart
so is he.* A man is not better than his thought-life! We
are what we think and what we think about will come
out in our lives.

Our feelings do follow our thoughts, and *as we think,
so we are.* Nothing is truer than this fact and nothing is
more absurd than the belief that we can hide our
thoughts from other people. It is how we tell ourselves
that as long as we do not express our thoughts in words,
nobody can possibly know anything about them and
they remain safely hidden.

Scriptures indicate that our mind is often the basis for
the difficulties and problems that we experience.

Now the mind of the flesh [which is sense and reason
without the Holy Spirit,] is death—death that com-

prises all the miseries arising from sin, both here and hereafter. But the mind of the (Holy) Spirit is life and soul-peace. . . . [That is] because the mind of the flesh —with its carnal thoughts and purposes—is hostile to God. . . .

Romans 8:6, 7 AMPLIFIED

God knows the content of our thoughts.

All the ways of a man are pure in his own eyes, but the Lord weighs the spirits—the thoughts and intents of the heart.

Proverbs 16:2 AMPLIFIED

For the Word that God speaks is alive and full of power —making it active, operative, energizing and effective; it is sharper than any two-edged sword, penetrating to the dividing line of the breath of life (soul) and [the immortal] spirit, and of joints and marrow [that is, of the deepest parts of our nature] exposing *and* sifting *and* analyzing *and* judging the very thoughts and purposes of the heart.

Hebrews 4:12 AMPLIFIED

He knows that man's mind is against God and in itself is incapable of changing. It is controlled by man's evil nature. The non-Christian's mind is so distorted that he cannot understand the truth.

So this I say and solemnly testify in [the name of] the Lord [as in His Presence], that you must no longer live as the heathen (the Gentiles) do in their perverseness —in the folly, vanity and emptiness of their souls and the futility—of their minds. Their moral understand-

ing is darkened *and* their reasoning is beclouded.
[They are] alienated (estranged, self-banished) from
the life of God—with no share in it. [This is] because
of the ignorance—the want of knowledge and perception, the willful blindness—that is deep-seated in
them, due to their hardness of heart (to the insensitive-
ness of their moral nature).

Ephesians 4:17, 18 AMPLIFIED

Because when they knew *and* recognized Him as
the God, they did not honor *and* glorify Him as God,
or give Him thanks. But instead they became futile
and godless in their thinking—with vain imaginings,
foolish reasoning and stupid speculations—and their
senseless minds were darkened.

Romans 1:21 AMPLIFIED

When a person becomes a Christian, God gives him
a new life through the new birth (*see* John 3). He
becomes a new creation (*see* 2 Corinthians 5:17) and
receives a new *capacity* of mind, heart, and will. Many
Christians struggle along with their previous pattern of
thinking and do not avail themselves of the new freedom and discipline available to them. By activating his
new mind and following the scriptural pattern for
thinking, a person will have the emotional freedom he
seeks. This scriptural pattern is found in several passages.

In Ephesians 4:23 Paul says to be *renewed in the
spirit of your mind.* This is allowing the spirit of the
mind to be controlled by the indwelling Holy Spirit.
The spirit of the mind is that which gives the mind the
discretion and content of its thought. The renewal here
is basically an act of God's Spirit powerfully influencing

man's spirit, his mental attitude, or state of mind.

Romans tells us *Do not be conformed to this world, but be transformed by the renewal of your mind . . .* (*see* verse 12:2). This passage is talking about a renovation, a complete change for the better. The word *renewal* here means *to make new from above.* Man's thoughts, imaginations, and reasonings are changed through the working of the Holy Spirit. As Dr. Bernard Ramm puts it, "The Spirit establishes the direct connection from the mind of God to the mind of the Christian."

The *first step* in controlling your thoughts comes from the ministry of the Holy Spirit in your life. This reflects, however, upon *your own willingness* to let the Holy Spirit work in your life and to stop trying to run your life by yourself. Renewal of the mind brings about a spiritual transformation in the life of the Christian.

The *second step* in the process is to consider the direction of your thought-life itself. What do you think about? As suggested by Proverbs 23:7, *What a man thinks in his heart, so is he.* As we build up storehouses of memories, knowledge, and experiences we seem to retain and remember those things which we concentrated upon the most. We are largely responsible for the things we let our minds dwell upon. We are told in Philippians 4:8 RSV just what we are to think about.

Finally, brethren, whatever is true, whatever is honorable, whatever is just, whatever is pure, whatever is lovely, whatever is gracious, if there is any excellence, if there is anything worthy of praise, think about these things.

What do these words mean in terms of our thought-life? The word *true* means just that. There are many concepts, philosophies, and assumptions that are deceptive and illusory. The content of our thoughts should be those things that we can rely on, those things that will not let us down.

Honorable is a difficult word to describe or translate. It actually refers to that which has the dignity of holiness about it. Many thoughts appear attractive but are really flimsy and cheap. The idea in this verse is that we should set our minds upon those things that are more serious and dignified.

In the New Testament the word *just* means a state of right being or right conduct. It is also used to describe people who are faithful in fulfilling their duty to God and to men. Our thoughts ought then to be on those things which would lead to proper conduct as well as proper thinking about our duty to God and man.

Pure describes that which is morally pure, free from defilement and contamination. So often a person's thoughts become degraded because he dwells on negative and dirty ideas. Our thoughts ought to be clean.

The word *lovely* means pleasing, agreeable or winsome—thoughts of kindness, love, and acceptance as opposed to vengeful or bitter ones. How we think of others can determine how we act toward them. If the mind of the Christian is set on lovely thoughts his actions will reflect the pattern of Christian behavior.

Gracious means of good report or fair-speaking. Perhaps it can imply that the words that go through our own minds should reflect fairness and should be words that we would not be hesitant to have God or men hear.

The word *think* means to consider, ponder, or to let

one's mind dwell on. Colossians 3:2 advises that we should set our minds and keep them set on what is above—the higher things—not on the things that are on the earth. As A. W. Tozer in *Born After Midnight* writes:

. . . Thinking about God and holy things creates a moral climate favorable to the growth of faith and love and humility and reverence. We cannot by thinking add one cubit to our stature or make evil good or darkness light. So to teach is to misrepresent a scriptural truth and to use it to our own undoing. But we can by Spirit-inspired thinking help to make our minds pure sanctuaries in which God will be pleased to dwell.

The *third step* is to realize that the Christian *does not* have to be dominated by the thinking of the old mind, the old pattern. He has been set free. *God has not given us the spirit of fear, but of power, and of love, and of a sound mind* (*see* 2 Timothy 1:7). Soundness means that the new mind can do what it is supposed to do. It can fulfill its function.

The *fourth step* is to let your mind be filled with the mind of Christ. There are three Scripture passages which place definite responsibility upon the Christian in this regard. In Philippians 2:5 KJV, Paul commands, *Let this mind be in you, which was also in Christ Jesus.* This could be translated, *Be constantly thinking this in yourselves* or *Reflect in your own minds, the mind of Christ Jesus.* The meaning here for the words *this mind be* is "to have understanding, to be wise, to direct one's mind to a thing, to seek or strive for" (*see* Wuest's Word Studies in *The Greek New Testament* for explanation).

The main thrust here is for the Christian to emulate in his life the virtues of Jesus Christ as presented in the previous three verses.

> Complete my joy by being of the same mind. . . . Do nothing from selfishness or conceit, but in humility count others better than yourselves. Let each of you look not only to his own interests, but also to the interests of others.
>
> Philippians 2:2–4 RSV

In verses six through eight another example of Christ is given—that of humility. This humility came about through submission to the will of God. The mind of Christ knew God and submitted to Him. A Christian following Jesus Christ must give his mind in submission to God.

A second passage, 2 Peter 1:13, tells us to *gird up your minds.* The words refer to mental exertion, putting out of the mind anything that would hinder progress in the Christian experience. Thoughts of worry, fear, lust, hate, jealousy, and unforgiveness, are to be eliminated from the mind. Nowhere in Scripture does it say we are to get rid of these thoughts *if we feel like it* or tell someone else to get rid of them. The responsibility is upon the individual. It takes effort, determination, and a desire to be rid of these emotions or thoughts. When the desire is there, the ministry of the Holy Spirit is available to assist. Through the work of the Holy Spirit a person can exert his will over those thoughts that work against the Christian life.

Herman Gockel writes in *Answer to Anxiety* about this process.

There is much more to this whole business than merely getting rid of negative or unworthy thoughts. In fact, the concept of "getting rid" is itself a sign of negative thinking. We shall succeed in this whole matter, not in the measure in which we empty our minds of sinful and degrading thoughts, but rather in the measure in which we *fill* them with thoughts that are wholesome and uplifting. The human mind can never be a vacuum. He who thinks he can improve the tenants of his soul simply by evicting those that are unworthy will find that for every unworthy tenant he evicts through the back door several more will enter through the front (see Matthew 12:43–45). It is not merely a matter of evicting. It is also a matter of screening, selecting, admitting, and cultivating those tenants that have proved themselves desirable.

This is the pattern set forth in Philippians 4:6–8 which tells us what to *stop* thinking about and what to *begin* thinking about.

Many Christians fail to bring into their minds the proper thoughts. Others hold onto the old pattern of thinking while they attempt to bring in the new pattern of thought. The result is conflict.

A third passage, 2 Corinthians 10:3–5, talks about *casting down every vain imagination* and *bringing every thought captive*. Imagination is the deduction of man's reason. Every thought that would be contrary to the Christian way of life is to be eliminated. Every thought should be brought into subjection to Jesus Christ.

The *fifth step* is this: In order to sustain the new thinking pattern it is important for the Christian to fill his mind with those thoughts and resources which will help him. Scripture itself fills this need.

> How can a young man keep his way pure? By guarding it according to thy word. With my whole heart I seek thee; let me not wander from thy commandments! I have laid up thy word in my heart, that I might not sin against thee.
>
> Psalms 119:9–11 RSV

We are also told to *desire the sincere milk of the word, that you may grow (see* 1 Peter 2:2). The Word of God is the safeguard against sins of the mind. Solomon said to commit your works upon the Lord. *(He will cause your thoughts to become agreeable to His will) so shall your plans be established and succeed (see* Proverbs 16:3 AMPLIFIED). An attitude of yielding and dependence upon God is a first step.

A person who reads, studies, and memorizes the Word of God will find it easier to think and act according to the pattern it sets forth, as Webb Garrison writes in "The Joy of Memorizing Scripture."

A "mind set" is slowly molded by Scripture that is memorized and often repeated. Anyone who devotes as much as fifteen minutes a day to this process for several years undergoes subtle changes. Most of them occur so gradually that he is hardly aware of them.

David Augsburger suggests in *Seventy Times Seven:*

Read the Bible. Mull it over. Let it soak down deep into your mind. Memorize it. There is power in stocking your memory and your heart with what is lovely, good, wholesome, true (cf. Philippians 4:8).

The truth of God absorbed into the mind and heart can act as a disinfectant to deal with the accumulated infections of our sinfulness.

The Word of God stored within a mind is a strengthening factor.

In addition to studying the Word of God, the *sixth step* is to strengthen our minds through prayer.

> Have no anxiety about anything, but in everything by prayer and supplication with thanksgiving let your requests be made known to God. And the peace of God, which passes all understanding, will keep your hearts and minds in Christ Jesus.
>
> Philippians 4:6,7 RSV

> Hitherto you have asked nothing in my name; ask, and you will receive, that your joy may be full.
>
> John 16:24 RSV

> Ask, and it will be given you; seek and you will find; knock, and it will be opened to you. For every one who asks receives, and he who seeks finds, and to him who knocks it will be opened.
>
> Matthew 7:7, 8 RSV

God will keep our minds and He will answer us. But it is up to us to ask.

The new birth is the starting point for our emotional control. Bringing our thoughts under the control of the Holy Spirit is the final step.

The following story from Augsburger's *Seventy Times Seven* illustrates something of the part emotions play in our lives and the control which is possible through the Holy Spirit (*italics* added).

> There was once a tiger keeper and a tiger cub who lived together. The keeper wanted the tiger for a pet, a friend. He fed him, walked him, cared for him. He always spoke

softly, warmly to him. But as the tiger grew, his green eyes began to glow with hostility. His muscles rippled their warning of power. One night, when the keeper was off guard, a lovely girl happened by. The claws reached out. There was a scream. The keeper arrived too late. Then others felt the tiger's teeth—a boy, a man. And the keeper in panic prayed that the tiger might die, but still he lived. In fear, the keeper caged him in a deep, dark hole where no one could get near. Now the tiger roared night and day. The keeper could not work or sleep through the roars of his guilt. Then he prayed that God might tame the tiger. God answered, "Let the tiger out of the cave. I will give you strength to face him." The keeper, willing to die, opened the door. The tiger came out. They stood. Stared. When the tiger saw no fear in the keeper's eyes, he lay down at his feet. Life with the tiger began. At night he would roar, but the keeper would look him straight in the eye, face him again and again. The tiger was never completely in his power, although as years passed they became friends. The keeper could touch him. But he never took his eyes off him, or off God who gave him the strength to tame the beast. Only then was he free from the roar of remorse, the growl of guilt, the raging of his own evil.

Both keeper and tiger are you.

God has not offered to kill your tiger. Death will do that all too soon. But His offer is and has been the strength to tame that evil within. To master it, before it masters you. He can and will set you free from its tyranny.

Then He supplies the strength to live with your own passions, lusts, hostilities in check, so that the true you, made in God's own image, begins to live. And what a change. Christ called it a new birth. *It's all that and more!*

4
Worry and Anxiety—Man's Private War

Death was walking towards a city and a man stopped
Death and said, "What are you going to do?" Death
said, "I'm going to kill ten thousand people." The
man said, "That's horrible!" Death said, "That's the
way it is, that's what I do." So the day passed and the
man met Death coming back. He said, "You said you
were going to kill ten thousand people and there
were 70 thousand killed." Death said, "Well I only
killed ten thousand. Worry and fear killed the others."

AUTHOR UNKNOWN

Not all wars are fought between nations or individuals. Every person has the capacity of carrying on his
own individual war with himself. This individual holo-
caust is called anxiety, for anxiety or worry is the state
of being at war with oneself. The writer of the Book of
Proverbs described this conflict by saying *Anxiety in a
man's heart weighs him down (see* verse 12:25). The
Greeks described anxiety as opposing forces at work to
tear a man apart.

When people talk about anxiety they often associate
it with the word *fear.* Fear is an emotion and like all
emotions it contains energy. This energy is often expressed in the form of an impulse to do something.

49

There are many words that describe fear: anxiety, dismay, worry, apprehension, timidity, shyness, dread, fright, alarm, panic, terror, and horror. When the presence of fear is found in a person we may say that he is: afraid, anxious, alarmed, nervous, apprehensive, worried, upset, disturbed, scared, fainthearted, shy, timid, bashful, diffident, modest, frightened, fearful, or aghast.

But there is a big difference between fear and anxiety or worry. Fear is an emotional response which is consciously recognized and it is usually stimulated by a real threat or a problem. There is a good reason why the person should be afraid. If you are driving down a freeway and suddenly a car heads directly for you toward a head-on collision, fear would be a very appropriate reaction. If you are traveling on a plane across the Atlantic and the engines fail and the plane begins to scream toward the water, the fear you experience would be legitimate. If a prowler lurking in the darkness of a room in your home lunges toward you with a knife you would probably experience fear. All of the fear reactions mentioned here are proper because there is a real danger.

What then is anxiety? It is a feeling of dread, apprehension, or uneasiness which produces a sense of approaching danger but it does not always stem from a reasonable cause. It is a state of acute fear and is often continuous. Many people experience what are called *anxiety states;* they feel apprehensive or uneasy but they cannot pin down any cause or reason. Many anxiety states stem from early childhood experiences or incidents which seemingly come back to haunt the person with feelings of dread. Anxiety appears to arise in response to some danger or threat, yet often the source of this impending doom is not clear. Much of the anxiety that people experience can be described as fear in the absence of an adequate cause. Some anxiety is experienced when the fear response is out of proportion to the so-called danger.

Worry is often associated with anxiety. Worry is a state of fearfulness and it too can be tied into a problem or situation, either imagined or real. There is no sharp line of separation between *worry* and *anxiety*. The words are often used interchangeably.

The word *worry* actually means to fret or be overly concerned. Persons who worry spend great quantities of time thinking and dwelling upon real or imagined problems. They go over and over them in their minds. They usually begin thinking the worst about the situation and they cross many bridges before they ever get to them. The word comes from a combination of two words which mean *mind* and *divide*. Worry means literally to divide the mind. Intense worry is about as useful in thinking as lighted matches in a dynamite factory.

John Haggai in his book *How To Win Over Worry* has suggested the following description.

Worry divides the feelings, therefore the emotions lack stability. Worry divides the understanding, therefore convictions are shallow and changeable. Worry divides the faculty of perception, therefore observations are faulty and even false. Worry divides the faculty of judging, therefore attitudes and decisions are often unjust. These decisions lead to damage and grief. Worry divides the determinative faculty, therefore plans, and purposes, if not "scrapped" altogether, are not filled with persistence.

More often than not a state of worry can be tied down to some source whether it is really a danger or not. Any situation which constitutes a threat (whether real or imagined) to one's self or a loved one can be a source of worry. A person who becomes a chronic worrier will experience anxiety, even to the extent of the anxiety states mentioned earlier.

Is all worry and anxiety bad? Is there any creative aspect to these reactions? Cecil Osborne in *The Art of Understanding Yourself* observes that

> . . . not all anxiety is destructive. There is a creative form of anxiety which causes a man to get out of bed in the morning and go to work. A mother answers the cry of her child in response to an inner anxiety which is also creative. [Sudden danger] stimulates the secretion of additional adrenalin into the bloodstream and prepares us for "fight or flight." This is a God-given instinctual response to fear. It is only when fear becomes an all-pervasive anxiety which impairs our effectiveness that it ceases to be creative and becomes destructive.

Dr. Quentin Hyder suggests in *The Christian's Handbook of Psychiatry:*

> All anxiety or psychic tension is not bad however. A little of it in normal amounts can enhance performance. Athletes would be unable to perform successfully without it. Businessmen do better in their competitive world than they could do without its stimulus. It definitely strengthens concentration and spurs imagination, thereby producing more creative ideas. It stimulates interest and develops ambition. It protects from danger. Too much, however, can actually decrease performance.

These men have been talking about anxiety in its healthy form. Worry, however, has no such creative element. But isn't there such a thing as concern? Is it the same as worry? Dr. Samuel Kraines and E. Thetford in *Help for the Depressed* distinguish between the two in this way.

Concern is often good and desirable. Concern is usually focused on a specific problem (will my son be drafted, will my daughter marry the right man, or will there be a general economic depression). Although a sense of fear is present in "concern" there is primarily uneasiness, unhappiness, and greater personal identification with the problem than with pure fear states. Such concern often leads to attempts at a solution of the problem; if my son goes to college, he may be deferred from military service. If I give many parties, will my daughter have a better chance of meeting the right person? If I write to my congressman about overspending, will that help ward off a business depression?

Worry, however, is primarily apprehension [fear], agitation [fear], and anxiety [fear], with relatively little self-control. "Concern" binds man to man and furnishes the motive power that stimulates corrective action. Worry turns inward and often paralyzes action. (From Kraines, Samuel H. and Thetford, Eloise S., HELP FOR THE DEPRESSED, 1972. Courtesy of Charles C Thomas, Publisher, Springfield, Illinois.)

Another description is expressed by a pastor, as Earl Lee writes in *The Cycle of Victorious Living:*

Tension is normal and natural in life. Without tension we could not exist any more than a violin string can be played without being stretched across the bridge. This creative tension is not the same thing as destructive worry. Worry is like racing an automobile engine while it is in neutral. The gas and noise and smog do not get us anywhere. But legitimate concern (creative tension) is putting the car into low gear on your way to moving ahead. You tell yourself that you are going to use the power God has given you to do something about the situation which could cause you to fret.

Worry immobilizes a person and does not lead to action. Concern moves to overcome the problem.

What are the causes of anxiety? What do most people worry about? Much anxiety can be attributed to repressed hostility. Having unrealistic standards set for us or setting them ourselves can create this tension. Situations in which a person must make a choice create anxiety. So does unresolved or undealt-with guilt. In *The Dynamics of Personal Adjustment* Lehner and Kube suggest that anxiety may stem from

. . . the discrepancies between an individual's level of achievement, and the goals and rewards a society regards as desirable. Thus an individual who is a member of a society that stresses material wealth and status may become anxious, worried, and distraught if he fails to make a lot of money and to improve his social position. This will be true especially if his close friends and associates expect him to achieve these goals. . . . The need to express aggressiveness or hostility may also be a source of anxiety, when such expression is stifled by cultural restrictions or threatening consequences. . . . Indeed, any demands with which the individual feels he cannot cope or that are in conflict with his needs can be sources of anxiety.

What do people worry about? It would be safe to say *everything.* Dr. Kraines suggests the three categories into which most worries fall.

1. Disturbing situations for which one must find a solution; for example, how to obtain money for food, lodging, or medical expenses.
2. Disturbing situations over which one has no control; for example, a mother dying of cancer; a usually prompt daughter who is five hours "late"; or a son in active combat.
3. Unimportant, insignificant, minor problems of everyday life which warrant little attention, let alone "worry." People "worry" about minor details of everyday life, concocting horrible possibilities, and then "stewing" about them. The housewife "worries" that she cannot clean the house as she once did, does not iron the clothes well, and cannot prepare proper meals. The man 'worries' that he is doing poorly at work, that he will be "fired" and that he "cannot pay his bills." The list goes on and on. The worry is not only a feeling tone of fearfulness but an overriding sense of futility, hopelessness, and dreaded possibilities. (From Kraines, Samuel H. and Thetford, Eloise S., HELP FOR THE DEPRESSED, 1972. Courtesy of Charles C Thomas, Publisher, Springfield, Illinois.)

What are the results of anxiety or worry? What do we actually accomplish? Regarding anxiety, Dr. Hyder says that:

Too much, however, can actually decrease performance. It can dampen reasoning abilities, dull imaginative thinking, cause discouragement, and take the joy and peace out of a person's life. It can also cause psychosomatic symptoms like an upset stomach, palpitations of the heart, headaches, cramped muscles, and a variety of vague aches and pains all over the body.

J. Macdonald Wallace in his book *Relaxation, A Key to Better Living* describes the physical "alarm reaction" which accompanies emotions of anxiety, fear or anger. These reactions begin in a portion of the brain called the hypothalamus. The alarm is triggered off in the hypothalamus, and a whole host of things happen. From the motor area, signals are sent to muscles to tense, ready to fight or to flee—as many muscles and as much tension, as the situation seems to require. Instantly, from the hypothalamus, urgent signals are sent by the sympathetic nervous system to all other systems to bolster up the muscles in their readiness. The heart beats faster and more strongly; breathing becomes quicker and more shallow; tiny blood vessels contract to shut off the blood supply from the digestive system and direct it to the active muscles; the muscular walls of the gullet, the stomach and the intestines may go into spasm, producing the nauseating feeling of "butterflies"; blood pressure is raised; the sweat glands open up, and the salivary glands dry up; more red blood cells are pumped into the circulating blood from the spleen in order to supply more oxygen to the muscles, and more sugar is released from the liver to supply the necessary energy to the muscles. Vomiting or urination may occur. At the same time, an instant signal is sent to the adrenal gland to release more adrenalin into the bloodstream. The adrenalin continues to maintain all the above reactions which were initiated by the sympathetic nervous system.

There are many scriptural references and descriptions of the effects of fear and anxiety.

I heard, and my [whole inner self] trembled, my lips quivered at the sound. Rottenness enters into my bones and under me—down *to my feet*—I tremble.

Habakkuk 3:16 AMPLIFIED

Anxiety in a man's heart weighs it down.

Proverbs 12:25 AMPLIFIED

A tranquil mind gives life to the flesh.

Proverbs 14:30 RSV

All the days of the desponding afflicted are made evil [by anxious thoughts and foreboding], but he who has a glad heart has a continual feast [regardless of circumstances].

Proverbs 15:15 AMPLIFIED

A happy heart is a good medicine and a cheerful mind works healing, but a broken spirit dries the bones.

Proverbs 17:22 AMPLIFIED

A glad heart makes a cheerful countenance, but by sorrow of heart the spirit is broken.

Proverbs 15:13 AMPLIFIED

The final results of anxiety are negative, self-defeating, and incapacitating. What do we accomplish by worrying? Are there any positive results? Make a list of the things you worry about and then describe specifically what the worry has or will accomplish. Does it solve the problem—or does it create *more* problems? When a person worries about a problem, real or imaginary, it usually impedes him from being able to do something effective about the problem.

Worrying intensely about the possibility of some event happening not only *does not prevent it* from happening but can help to bring it about! A young seminary student is waiting to preach his first sermon. He sits thinking about what he is going to say. He begins to worry about forgetting words, about stumbling over certain phrases, and not presenting himself in a confident manner. As he continues to worry he actually visualizes himself making these mistakes. He actually sees himself failing, and the more he goes over and over this in his mind the more mistakes he sees himself making as he anticipates getting up to preach this sermon. And then when he does get up to preach he actually *does* make those mistakes that he worried about! If you were to tell him that he shouldn't worry about his preaching he would reply, "I was justified in worrying. After all, those problems that I worried about were real problems. They happened, didn't they? I *should* have been worried!" What he does not realize is that by his own worry he actually helped them occur. He was responsible for his failure. He spent more time seeing himself failing than he did visualizing himself succeeding or overcoming the problem.

The principle here is that if you spend time seeing yourself as a failure or failing you will more than likely follow that example in your performance. You actually condition yourself for that kind of performance because of your negative thinking. However, if you spend that same amount of time and energy planning how to overcome those anticipated mistakes and visualize yourself being successful, your performance will be far better. Our thinking pattern affects how we perform. Proverbs says that *As a man thinketh in his heart so is he* (*see* verse 23:7).

People who worry about having an accident when they are driving on the freeway are very accident-prone. They are actually more likely to have accidents than others because they constantly visualize the event.

What we must remember is that overconcern, worry in this instance, about a problem or potentially dangerous situation usually exaggerates the chances of its actually occurring. Why? Because the energy used in worry is not directed toward solving the problem. The classic example is the person who worries about getting an ulcer and in a few months he is rewarded for his efforts.

Does worry have any place in the life of the Christian? Is worry or anxiety a sin? A slight amount of anxiety or tension, as mentioned earlier, is healthy. A person, however, who experiences extreme states of anxiety may not be able to control them. There may be many deep hidden feelings or hurts that have lingered for years and move about in the unconscious. On the one hand the person may feel he is at the mercy of these feelings because he cannot pin down exactly why he is so anxious. However, if a person suffers from anxiety for very long, perhaps there may be a problem of sin because he has failed to face the problem, discover the roots of his feelings, and replace them with the healing power and resources offered through Jesus Christ and Scripture.

Anxiety may stem from unconscious feelings. Worry, however, is a conscious choosing of an ineffective method of coping with life. Oswald Chambers has said that all our fret and worry is caused by calculating without God. Worry actually implies the absence of trust. Since Scripture gives such direct answers to the problem of worry and actually tells us not to worry, this lack of trust in the Lord is certainly sin. *Freedom from worry is possible. The answer lies in Scripture.*

Therefore I tell you, stop being perpetually uneasy (anxious and worried) about your life, what you shall eat *or what you shall drink,* and about your body, what you shall put on. Is not life greater [in quality] than food, and the body [far above and more excellent] than clothing? Look at the birds of the air; they neither sow nor reap nor gather into barns, and yet your heavenly Father keeps feeding them. Are you not worth more than they? And which of you by worrying *and* being anxious can add one unit of measure [cubit] to his stature *or* to the span of his life? And why should you be anxious about clothes? Consider the lilies of the field *and* learn thoroughly how they grow; they neither toil nor spin; Yet I tell you, even Solomon in all his magnificence (excellence, dignity and grace) was not arrayed like one of these. But if God so clothes the grass of the field, which today is alive *and* green and tomorrow is tossed into the furnace, will He not much more surely clothe you, O you men with little faith? Therefore do not worry *and* be anxious, saying, What are we going to have to eat? or, What are we going to have to drink? or, What are we going to have to wear? For the Gentiles (heathen) wish for *and* crave *and* diligently seek after all these things; and your heavenly Father well knows that you need them all. But seek for (aim at and strive after) first of all His kingdom, and His righteousness [His way of doing and being right], and then all these things taken together will be given you besides. So do not worry *or* be anxious about tomorrow, for tomorrow will have worries *and* anxieties of its own. Sufficient for each day is its own trouble.

Matthew 6:25–34, AMPLIFIED

From this passage we can discover several principles to help us overcome anxiety and worry. First, note that

Jesus did *not say,* "If everything is going all right for you and there are no problems then stop worrying." He did *not say,* "If you feel like it then do not worry." He simply and directly said to stop worrying about your life. Perhaps in a way Jesus was saying that we should learn to accept situations that cannot be altered at the present time. This does not mean that we are to sit back and make no attempt to improve conditions around us, but we must face them and admit that this is the way they are. Learn how to live with them for the present.

Second, Jesus said that you cannot add any length of time to your life by worry. *But you can take years off your life by worry and anxiety!* The physical result of worry can actually shorten your life-span.

A third suggestion made is that what we worry about may be part of the difficulty. It could be that our sense of values is distorted and that what we worry about should not be the center of our attention. The material items that seem so important should be secondary.

Christ also recommends that we practice living a day at a time. It is not possible to relive the past or to change what occurred in the past. Perhaps some of the results of the past can be changed but some cannot. At any rate, worry certainly is not the solution. Nor is it possible to predict the future. We can prepare as best as possible for it but even then we still must wait. The effect of worry will inhibit the potential of what can occur in the future. Past experience does indicate several factors concerning worry. First of all, most of the events about which people worry do not happen. Look at the list of items you have worried over. Did they ever happen? Of course, now and then a person will say, "Yes, every one of these came true." Perhaps the reason for that is because of the worry. If you worried about failing, your energy was directed toward failing.

A second element of worry is that the anticipation of certain events that are inevitable usually is more distressing than the actual experience. Someone has said that anticipation is the magnifying glass of the emotions.

And third, even if an event is as serious as its anticipation, it is possible to discover unsuspected resources to meet it. The Christian especially has resources for strength and stability at all times. Perhaps the manner in which we are able to be sustained in times of difficulty can be illustrated by looking at another passage of Scripture. In Matthew 14:22–33 we find the disciples in a boat and Jesus walking toward them on the water. Peter saw Jesus and He invited Peter to come to Him. So Peter began to walk toward Jesus. He was fine until he saw the wind and then he became afraid and started to sink. If Peter had kept his eyes and mind upon Christ (the source of strength and the solution) he would have been all right. But Peter focused upon the wind and the rising waves stirred up by the wind (the problem or the negative aspect). He became overwhelmed by the problem even though he could have made it safely to Jesus! Worry is like that. We focus so hard on the problem that we take our eyes off the solution and thus create more difficulties for ourselves. We can be sustained in the midst of any difficulty by relying upon Jesus Christ.

The important principle to remember from these two passages of Scripture is this: *We must learn to live a day at a time and accept certain situations and deal with them a step at a time. Worry should not be allowed as it does not solve the problem. And in the midst of our situation our main focus should be on Jesus Christ and not the difficulty.*

In 1 Peter 5:7 KJV another resource for worry is presented: *Casting all your care [or anxieties] upon Him; for He careth for you.* This passage tells us what we are to do and then why we are to do it. Cast means to give up, or as one translation puts it *Unload all your cares on Him.* Cast actually means "having deposited with" and refers here to a direct and once-for-all committal to God of all that would give a person concern. The word *care* means anxiety or worry. All worries are to be cast upon the Lord so that when problems arise in the future that would have caused us to worry we will not worry about them. The reason we can cast these cares on God with confidence is that God cares for us. We can be certain that, because He cares for us, He will strengthen us. He is not out to break us down but to help us stand firm. He knows our limits. *A bruised reed He will not break, and a dimly burning wick He will not quench* (Isaiah 42:3 RSV).

The principle of this verse is: **You can unload and give over every worry to God and because of His care and love He will strengthen you for any difficulty.**

Another Old Testament passage clarifies what a person should do if he is to be free of worry in his life. As in Isaiah 26:3, *He will keep you in perfect peace whose mind [or imagination] is stayed on thee.*

What we choose to think about will affect our actions and inner calmness. Those who suffer with worry *choose* to wrestle with negative thoughts or anticipate the worst. What goes on within our imagination creates the anxiety feelings. If your mind or imagination is centered about God—what He has done and will do for you —if it is centered upon the promises of Scripture, peace of mind is inevitable. But you must choose to center your thoughts in this way. God has made the provision but you must take the action. Freedom from worry and anxiety is available but you must lay hold of it. The principle here is: ***Learn to direct your thoughts toward God and His teachings and you will never need to worry.***

Psalms 37 KJV begins with the words *Fret not . . .* and those two words are repeated in later verses. The dictionary defines fret as "to eat away, gnaw, gall, vex, worry, agitate, wear away." One of the delights of the Word of God is that when God says not to do something or to stop something, a positive substitute is provided. This psalm makes four positive suggestions regarding worry or fretting. Verse three states *Trust in the Lord . . .* The Amplified Bible renders the word trust as *lean on, rely on, and be confident.* This is a matter of not attempting to live an independent life and cope with difficulties alone. It means going to a stronger source for strength. Verse four tells us to *delight* yourself in the Lord. Delight means to rejoice in God and what He has done for us. Let God be and supply the joy for your life.

Committing your way to the Lord is another one of the alternatives to fretting. Commitment is a definite act of the will and it involves releasing your worries and anxieties to the Lord. It is a complete flinging of one's self upon the Lord with no conditions or holding back. It means to dislodge the burden from your shoulders and lay it on God. It is part of the life of faith wherein we give ourselves to God, simply relying upon what we know of God as expressed in Scripture and not depending upon circumstances that we understand or can see visually.

The final suggestion is to rest in the Lord and wait patiently for Him. This word *rest* has a rich meaning. The Hebrew means "to cease, be silent, or submit in silence to what He ordains." But this involves a readiness and expectation for what God is going to bring and do in your life.

The principle in this psalm is: *Give up fretting and replace it with trusting God, relying upon Him to provide and expect Him to do so. Release yourself completely to Him.*

A clear pattern for the reduction and elimination of anxiety is given in Philippians 4:6, 7:

> Do not worry about anything; but in everything with prayer and supplication with thanksgiving let your requests be made known to God. And the peace of God, which surpasses all human thought, will stand sentinel or guard over your hearts and minds in Christ Jesus.
>
> *Daily Study Bible*, William Barclay, Editor

The people to whom Paul wrote these words had many problems and had developed the pattern of worrying. Paul was very direct when he wrote to them. His words *Do not worry about anything* mean not even *one* thing. We are not asked to stop worrying if we feel like it or can see our way clear. It requires a definite act on our part to cease doing it.

But it isn't a matter of just stopping, without replacing this action with a positive substitute. If a person who has been accustomed to worrying stops but does not fill that void with something else he will revert back to his practice of worrying. People cannot exist in a vacuum. They must be doing something. Paul suggests something simple. He says that in everything with prayer and supplication with thanksgiving your requests should be made known unto God. There is no limit to what we can pray about. The most insignificant concern can be brought to God and He will respond. We can pray for forgiveness for the past, for what we need in the present, and for help and guidance for the future. Take your past, present, and future with all your shame, your needs, and your fears into the presence of God. And do it with thanksgiving. You might even include thanks for the actual privilege of prayer. We can give thanks in time of laughter or tears, in times of distress and pain, as well as experiences of joy and delight.

There is a positive result to this practice of prayer. You will be given peace in your heart and mind. God's peace, like a sentinel or guard, will replace the worry and assist in keeping future worries away. This peace surpasses all human thought or understanding. It does not mean that this peace is such a mystery that man's mind cannot understand it—although that is partly true. It does mean that the peace of God is so complete and valuable that man's mind, with all its skill and its knowledge and all its understanding can never construct it on its own or discover it or produce it. It is another one of the wonderful gifts from God.

The passage in Philippians can be divided into three basic stages. We are given the premise—*Do not worry.* We are told what to practice—*prayer.* And then we are given the promise—*peace.* It is there—available—but we must follow the first two steps in order for the third to occur. The principle of these verses is: **Stop worrying, start praying, and begin receiving God's peace which replaces the worry.**

The results of prayer as a substitute for worry can be vividly seen in two Old Testament passages. In Psalms 34 RSV David, who was undergoing a crisis in his own life, begins: *I will bless the Lord at all times; his praise shall continually be in my mouth.* David had just escaped from the Philistines who had captured him. He had faked the role of a madman knowing that they would release him rather than kill him. He then fled and hid in the cave of Adullam along with four hundred men who are described as men who were in distress, discontented, and in debt. In the midst of all this David wrote this psalm of praise. He did not say he would sometimes praise the Lord, but would do so *at all times*. No exception! This must have been a fearful time for David, knowing that the enemy was still after him. In verse four RSV he says, *I sought the Lord and he answered me, and delivered me from all my fears*. David had neither fear, worry, nor anxiety. He prayed and gave the problem over to God who lifted it away. Nor did David turn around and take these cares back after he had deposited them with the Lord. He gave them up. Too many people give their burdens to God with a rubber band attached. As soon as they stop praying the problems bounce back. Some people pray, *Give us this day our daily bread*, and then when they are through praying begin to worry where their next meal is going to come from.

Another factor to remember here is that God did not take David away from his problem. He was still in the cave with four hundred disgruntled men and he was still hiding. God does not always take us out of a problem situation but he gives us the peace that we are seeking as we proceed through that experience. It happened to David and it happens today for those who pray, unload their cares on God, and leave them there.

In the verse from Habakkuk quoted earlier in this chapter, the prophet expresses his fear. *When I heard, my belly trembled; my lips quivered at the voice: rottenness entered into my bones, and I trembled in myself....* God had told him of what was going to happen and what the Chaldeans were going to do. And the prophet was now in such a state of fear that he was unable to control his physical reactions. Try as hard as he could, he could not stop trembling. In the book *From Fear to Faith* by Dr. Martyn Lloyd-Jones the answer to this fear is given.

Instead of mere resignation, or plucking up one's courage, the Scripture shows that it is possible even under such conditions to be in a state of actual rejoicing. "Although the fig tree shall not blossom, neither shall fruit be in the vines; the labour of the olive shall fail, and the fields shall yield no meat; the flock shall be cut off from the fold, and there shall be no herd in the stalls: yet I will rejoice in the Lord, I will joy in the God of my salvation" [Habakkuk 3:17, 18 KJV]. The Christian claims nothing less than that. Your man of the world may, if he is in a physically good condition, school himself to a state of resignation. He may put on a courageous air as many did during the last war, and as many will continue to do. And that as far as it goes is a commendable spirit. But, in contrast to that, the Christian is assured that though he may be a person who is physically disposed to be thoroughly alarmed, he may experience not only strength but positive joy in the midst of danger. He may "rejoice in tribulation" and be triumphant in the midst of the worst circumstances. That is the challenge of the Christian position. Herein we as Christians are to differ from the world. When hell is let loose, and the worst comes to the worst, we are to do more than "put up with it" or "be steady." We are to know a holy joy and manifest a spirit of rejoicing. We are to be "more than conquerors," instead of merely exercising self-control with the aid of an iron will. We are to rejoice in the Lord and to joy in the God of our salvation. Such a time is a test for our Christian profession. If we are not then more than conquerors we are failing as Christians.

Now, what is it that makes this possible? The prophet finds his consolation in a right and Christian interpretation of history, to which reference has earlier been made. Whenever, in the Psalms, the writer faces situations such as we are envisaging, he invariably looks back at the history of God's dealings with men and thus finds himself praising God and rejoicing. The prophet likewise here reminds himself of certain of the great facts in the long story of the children of Israel, concentrating especially on the deliverance of Israel from the bondage in Egypt, their passage through the Red Sea, their journey through the wilderness, the defeat of their enemies and their occupation of Canaan.

We too must learn to employ this method. It may be that this will be the only thing that will hold us in the days that lie ahead. As we look out upon the world today is there any cause for rejoicing but this?

God has acted before throughout history and He acts today. The prophet learned to rejoice, to pray, and to rest in God. How is this possible for us today? The answer is in the Scriptures that have been discussed earlier. But they must be practiced and acted upon.

Both worry and anxiety are often panic reactions. The opposite of worry is faith and someone has suggested that faith is a refusal to panic. But in order to overcome your worry with faith you have to **activate your faith or put it into motion.** In Luke 8:22–25 KJV we find a situation where Jesus asked his disciples, *Where is your faith?* It is almost as though He were saying, "I know you have faith but where is it at this moment?" Faith has to be put into motion. Martyn Lloyd-Jones in his book *Spiritual Depression* suggests a way.

Faith is not something that acts automatically, faith is not something that acts magically. This, I think, is the blunder of which we have all, at some time or another, been guilty. We seem to think that faith is something that acts automatically. Many people, it seems to me, conceive of faith as if it were something similar to those thermostats which you have in connection with a heating apparatus, you set your thermostat at a given level, you want to maintain the temperature at a certain point and it acts automatically. If the temperature is tending to rise above that, the thermostat comes into operation and brings it down; if you use your hot water and the temperature is lowered, the thermostat comes into operation and sends it up, etc. You do not have to do anything about it, the thermostat acts automatically and it brings the temperature back to the desired level automatically. Now there are many people who seem to think that faith acts like that. They assume that it does not matter what happens to them, that faith will operate and all will be well. Faith, however, is not something that acts magically or automatically. If it did, these men would never have been in trouble, faith would have come into operation and they would have been calm and quiet and all would have been well. But faith is not like that and those are utter fallacies with respect to it.

What is faith? Let us look at it positively. The principle taught here is that faith is an activity, it is something that has to be exercised. It does not come into operation itself, you and I have to put it into operation. It is a form of activity.

When you find yourself in a difficult position the first thing to do is to refuse to allow yourself to be controlled by the situation or circumstances. Do not panic and do not look at just the problems facing you. The next step is to then remind yourself of what you believe and what you know to be true.

Your faith must be based upon the facts of Scripture and not your feelings. Faith holds onto truth and reasons from what it knows to be fact. That is the way faith acts but it must be exercised.

In order to live a life of faith and to overcome worry and anxiety you must focus upon and practice the definite promises of Scripture. When tempted to fear or worry, get out a biblical concordance or a topical Bible and look up all the verses on *fear*. Isaiah, for example, expressed many thoughts to uphold a person.

> Fear not, for I am with you, be not dismayed, for I am your God; I will strengthen you, I will help you, I will uphold you with my victorious right hand.
>
> Isaiah 41:10 RSV

> But now thus says the Lord, he who created you, O Jacob, he who formed you, O Israel: "Fear not, for I have redeemed you; I have called you by name, you are mine. When you pass through the waters I will be with you; and through the rivers, they shall not overwhelm you; when you walk through fire you shall not be burned, and the flame shall not consume you. For I am the Lord your God. . . .
>
> Isaiah 43:1–3 RSV

How to Deal With Worry and Anxiety

1. Be sure you have had a complete physical by your physician. Have him check glands, vitamin deficiencies, allergies, exercise schedule and fatigue.

2. Be aware of all of your emotions. Face your worries. Don't run from them for they will return to haunt you. Admit that you do worry or have anxiety (but only if you really

do). Do not worry about worrying. That just reinforces and perpetuates the problem.

3. Write down the worries and anxieties that you have on a piece of paper. Be very specific and complete as you describe them.

4. Write down the reason or cause for your worry. Investigate the source. *Is there any possibility that you can eliminate the source or cause for your worry? Have you tried? What have you tried specifically?*

5. Write down how much time you spend each day worrying.

6. What has your worry accomplished in your life? Describe in detail. Describe the benefits of worrying.

7. Make a list of the following:
(a.) How many times has my worrying prevented a situation from occurring?
(b.) In what way did my worry increase the problem?

8. If you are nervous or jumpy try to eliminate any sources of irritation. Stay away from situations that increase this until you learn how to react differently. Try to remove the source of irritation. For example, if the troubled world situation gets to you why listen to so many newscasts! What do you do to try to relax? Can you read, work in the garden, ride a bike for several miles? Avoid rushing yourself. If you worry about being late plan to arrive at a destination early. Give yourself more time.

9. Avoid any type of fatigue—physical, emotional, or intellectual. When a person is fatigued difficulties can loom out of proportion.

10. When you do get involved in worry is it over something that really pertains to you and your life *or* does it properly belong to someone else? Remember that often our

fears or worries may be disguised forms of the fear of what *others* think of us! (*See* H. Norman Wright, *Christian Marriage and Family Relationship.*)

11. When a problem arises, face it and make a decision as to what you can do about it. Make a list of all of the possible solutions and decide which you think is the best one. If these are minor decisions, make your decision fairly quickly, taking more time for major ones. A person who is a worrier usually says, "I can't decide. I go over and over these problems and cannot decide which is best." Look at the facts and then decide, but do not continue to worry about it. After you have looked at the facts and made your decision, do not question your choice. Otherwise the worrying pattern erupts all over again. Do not begin to debate your own decision. Practice this new pattern of making decisions. If you do fail in the beginning do not give up. Your old pattern has been locked in because of long use and you need to practice the new pattern of thinking for a while before it begins to work successfully. As soon as possible act upon your decision and get rid of the problem.

If it is a major problem it may be a difficult decision. As questions arise you may have to seek advice. Make a plan for obtaining this advice. It may take a day or a week, but when you have made the plans, dismiss the problem from your mind until that time, until you obtain the information you need. What good will it do to keep running over and over the problem until the time you gain this new information? With any kind of problem including those where the matter is out of your hands (such as the illness of a family member) you can leave the problem with the Lord. Do not carry the weight around on your own shoulders.

The Principles of Scripture

Matthew 6:25–34: *Learn how to live a day at a time.* Deal with your problems a step at a time. Do not allow worry to creep in. Focus upon Christ and not the problem. Write out a description of how you will put this into daily practice in your own life.

1 Peter 5:7: *Unload your worry on God and you will be strengthened* because of His love and care for you. Write down the specific cares and worries that you have at this time and then spend time in prayer giving these to the Lord.

Isaiah 26:3: *Direct your thoughts toward God and His teachings.* Describe how you will put this principle into practice in your life and how you will remember to do this each day.

Psalms 37: *Replace fretting with trust, delight, commitment and resting in the Lord.* Describe what each of these words means to you and how each one will help you release your worries and anxieties to God so you will be free of them.

Philippians 4:6,7: *Stop worrying, give everything to God in prayer and supplication and peace will be yours.* Describe how you need to pray for this to happen. Discuss the specific steps you will take to stop yourself from worrying.

5
Depression

The Lord is close to those who are of a broken heart, and saves such as are crushed with sorrow for sin *and* are humbly *and* thoroughly penitent.

Psalms 34:18 AMPLIFIED

At some time in our lives depression hits all of us. From the beginning of time man has cried out to God.

O Lord, the God of my salvation, I have cried to You for help by day; at night I am in Your presence. Let my prayer come before You *and* [really] enter into Your presence; incline Your ear to my cry! For I am full of troubles, and my life draws near to (Sheol) the place of the dead. I am counted among those who go down into the pit (the grave); I am as a man who has no help *or* strength—a mere shadow; cast away among the dead, like the slain that lie in a [nameless] grave, whom You (seriously) remember no more; and they are cut off from Your hand.

Psalms 88:1–5 AMPLIFIED

No one is immune to depression, not even the Christian. Some people experience depression on a shallow level while others dive to the depths of despondency. Some periods of depression last for a few hours, others linger on and on. Some end in suicide. Aaron T. Beck in *Depression: Causes and Treatment* describes how writers in ancient times often referred to depression as *melancholia.*

The first clinical description of melancholia was made by Hippocrates in the fourth century B.C. He also referred to swings similar to mania and depression (Jelliffe, 1931).

Aretaeus, a physician living in the second century, A.D., described the melancholic patient as "sad, dismayed, sleepless. . . . They become thin by their agitation and loss of refreshing sleep. . . . At a more advanced stage, they complain of a thousand futilities and desire death."

Plutarch, in the second century A.D., presented a particularly vivid and detailed account of melancholia:

> He looks on himself as a man whom the Gods hate and pursue with their anger. A far worse lot is before him; he dares not employ any means of averting or of remedying the evil, lest he be found fighting against the gods. The physician, the consoling friend, are driven away. "Leave me," says the wretched man, "me, the impious, the accursed, hated of the gods, to suffer my punishment." He sits out of doors, wrapped in sackcloth or in filthy rags. Ever and anon he rolls himself, naked, in the dirt confessing about this and that sin. He has eaten or drunk something wrong. He has gone some way or other which the Divine Being did not approve of. The festivals in honor of the gods give no pleasure to him but fill him rather with fear or a fright (quoted by Zilboorg 1941).

A depressed person has feelings of pessimism, discouragement or dejection. He may feel apathetic or despondent. Emotional exhaustion may set in and a preoccupation with life and misfortunes. Contemplation of suicide is a common result.

In depression there is real mental pain—a combination of anguish, despair, self-disgust, intense guilt with anger and fear. Hopelessness is a frequent companion. Depression affects us not only mentally but physically as well. Aches and pains, stomachache, pressure in the head and many other physical symptoms may occur. As Beck adds, depression may be defined in terms of the following attributes.

1. A specific alteration in mood: sadness, loneliness, apathy.
2. A negative self-concept associated with self-reproaches and self-blame.
3. Regressive and self-punitive wishes: desires to escape, hide, or die.
4. Vegetative changes: anorexia, insomnia, loss of libido.
5. Change in activity level: retardation or agitation.

Kinds of Depression

When one thinks of depression it is important to distinguish between the various kinds that plague people. Such a simple thing as not eating properly or not getting proper rest can cause depression. The person who does not eat regular meals or get sufficient sleep may find himself becoming depressed because he is cheating his body of the food and rest it needs to keep functioning properly. College students often suffer from this type of depression. The cure is simple and obvious: eat right and get enough sleep.

Reactions to certain drugs can affect a person's moods. Medications administered to correct a physical disturbance may cause a chemical change in the body that brings on the blues. All drugs affect the body and the mental processes in some way. If a drug results in brain or nervous system toxicity, extreme depression could be the result. If a person takes too much of a drug or sedative over an extended period of time he may be a candidate for toxic depression. The symptoms are listlessness, indifference, and difficulty in concentrating. Often the person evidences odd and illogical thought patterns which interfere with his normally good judgment. In many cases the depression and drug toxicity will clear up in a day or so after the drug is no longer in the system.

Infections of the brain or nervous system, generalized body infections, hepatitis and hypoglycemia can cause depression. Glandular disorders, a low thyroid condition, hyperthyroidism, excessive ovarian hormonal irregularities, and an imbalance of secretions from the adrenal or pituitary glands also cause a type of depression. Usually other symptoms and bodily changes are also in evidence.

Repressed anger turned inward upon oneself will lead to depression. In fact repressed anger is commonly used as a synonym for depression. This type of anger has been turned from its original source to the inner person. As William Blake wrote in "A Poison Tree":

> I was angry with my friend:
> I told my wrath, my wrath did end.
> I was angry with my foe:
> I told it not, my wrath did grow.

Reactive depression, usually called grief depression, immediately follows the loss of a loved one, a job or some important opportunity. The intensity of this type of depression is greater immediately after the loss and lessens as the weeks go by. During this time the person's usual functions of living may be impaired but he can still operate within normal limits. There is a sense of emptiness because of the loss. In some situations the person may feel guilty if he believes his own actions brought on the loss. For the most part, however, his feelings about himself and his self-esteem remain the same. We expect this type of grief depression when a person loses a loved one or even a close friend. Grief is very important in helping a person regain his full functioning capabilities.

Another major type of depression is biochemical or endogenous, generated internally. It is caused by a disturbance in the body's chemical system. Depression results when the brain and part of the nervous system become disorganized and no longer function normally. Only recently has endogenous depression been recognized as an organically caused disease. It seems to come from nowhere and in many cases appears to strike without warning. A person may have a fulfilling life with a happy marriage and excellent job but still be depressed.

There are two levels of endogenous depression. The symptoms in the first level are relatively mild and the person continues to work on a job or at home. But he is always tired no matter how much rest he gets. He loses enthusiasm and interest in usual activities. There is a change in his sleeping habits. He either gets more sleep than usual, or less. The sex desire and enjoyment lessen and his eating habits change. He loses his appetite and his weight drops. Many physical symptoms appear with no organic basis. The person worries about many things whether they are actual problems or not and states that he is just nervous, not really depressed. Short bursts of irritability with himself and others is another characteristic. Previous optimism has decreased to a discouraged pessimism. All of these symptoms fluctuate from day to day. *They do not change because of the environment but because of the chemical problem that exists.*

The second level of endogenous depression is much more intense. To the person experiencing this depression, it appears to be a terrible nightmare. He is excessively fearful and irritable. Feelings of hopelessness and suffering overwhelm him. His entire personality and his attitude toward life itself are disrupted. He suffers intense feelings of depression with crying spells for no apparent reason. Concentration is at an all-time low and he has difficulty making decisions—what to wear, what to eat, etc. He is interested in nothing except the turmoil that is going on inside him. Fears and phobias of disease, death, and suicide are very intense. He avoids other people, yet fears being left alone. He does not function normally in his work. Insomnia and a complete loss of appetite are common. Psychosomatic symptoms are present and an intense fear of these symptoms. He may believe he is insane and considers suicide. He does not go "crazy," however, and as hopeless as he may feel, recovery is definite and certain. Kraines and Thetford in *Help for the Depressed* advise that consultation with a physician is important to determine the type of depression and also the treatment. Medication, involvement with people, understanding the various kinds of depression and continuing the routine of daily living are important ingredients for recovery.

To understand the cause of endogenous depression

we must look at the brain. As we can see on page 82, the brain is divided into two parts: the cerebral cortex and the diencephalon. The cortex is like a thin skin covering the entire brain and acts like a computer. It is the human thinking machine. In a depressive illness this part of the brain is not involved. If it is sluggish it is because of the malfunction of the second portion of the brain. The second part is the core of the brain, the diencephalon, in which is located the hypothalamus which is the power source for the nervous system. This is, in effect, the emotional center. According to Dr. Kraines, endogenous depression results when this power center functions abnormally. When this center has too much energy you are excessively happy and full of life. When there is not sufficient energy you are fatigued and depressed.

As you look at the diagram you can see that the hypothalamus controls the nervous regulation of all organs: heart, stomach, bowels, colon, lungs. It also controls the autonomic nervous system which has two branches: the sympathetic system which speeds up bodily activity, and the parasympathetic system which slows it down.

The hypothalamus is also part of the system which takes nervous impulses to the cortex. These impulses represent how one *feels inside.* If the nervous impulses in this emotional circuit come from a body that is slow or sluggish in its functioning, with minimal influence of the sympathetic system (which speeds up the body), the sensations that go into the cortex are those of apathy, disinterest, and sluggishness. Therefore, the person is fatigued, disinterested, and unhappy. This happens because within the hypothalamus there is a chemical fuel called norepinephrine (NE). When there is too little of this fuel the emotional circuit is slowed down and the

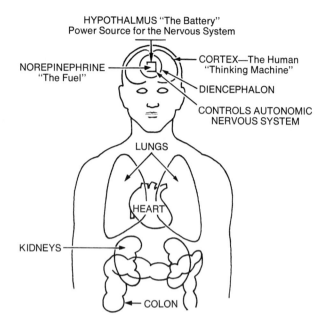

HYPOTHALMUS "The Battery"
Power Source for the Nervous System

NOREPINEPHRINE — "The Fuel"

CORTEX—The Human "Thinking Machine"

DIENCEPHALON

CONTROLS AUTONOMIC NERVOUS SYSTEM

LUNGS

HEART

KIDNEYS

COLON

person feels depressed. The less NE secreted, the slower the emotional circuit and the more depression results. (It should be remembered that other biochemical factors influence the nervous system too.)

In a sense the hypothalamus is like a battery and the fuel is the norepinephrine. The major supplier of nervous energy comes from the hypothalamus, and the cortex or *thinking machine* is operated in large part by this energy. When the battery is run down because of lack of fuel, the thinking machine is affected—the mind functions much slower than usual. And because the hypothalamus is connected to every organ in the body, when there is an imbalance in the autonomic nervous system every organ can be affected. Many physical symptoms can occur, from numbness of the skin to pressure in the head. There is nothing wrong with the organs—the problem lies with the malfunction of the hypothalamus. No one knows what brings about the biochemical change that decreases the amount of available norepinephrine. Studies have merely indicated that there is a drop in the NE level.

What can be done for the person who suffers from this type of depression? Kraines and Thetford have suggested some aspects of the problem.

It is important for depressive patients—and their relatives—to understand that the depressive mood and all the multiple, miserable symptoms that go along with it are the result of this physical loss of hypothalamic energy. No matter how good one's philosophy, no matter how well adjusted one has been, and no matter how ideal the environment may be, when there is a loss of hypothalamic energy, the person is depressed, feels helpless, and has no energy. If the depressed patient is very poor, giving him a million dollars will not make him happy. If the wealthy man has a depression, solving his problems with his business, his wife, his children, his arthritis, and his status will not cure his depression. Only a return of normal neurohormonal energy in the hypothalamus can effect a resolution of the depressive mood.
(From Kraines, Samuel H. and Thetford, Eloise S., HELP FOR THE DEPRESSED, 1972. Courtesy of Charles C Thomas, Publisher, Springfield, Illinois.)

Care from a physician, time, and patience are necessary to treat this kind of depression. If you are depressed remember that it is important to consider *all* possible causes. Do not simply assume that your depression is endogenous when the reason could be drugs, disease, or poor sleeping and eating habits. It could also be the result of faulty thinking which has long been considered a major contributor to depression. Psychiatrist Aaron T. Beck reports:

Robert Burton, writing in the seventeenth century, quoted numerous writers from antiquity to the seventeenth century who believed that the "afflictions of the mind" produced depression. In 1600 Felix Platter described depression or melancholia as "a kind of mental alienation, in which imagination and judgment are so perverted that without any cause the victims become very sad and fearful." He emphasized that the illness "rests upon a foundation of false conceptions."

Beck adds that among contemporary writers the role of the thinking person in depression is receiving more and more emphasis. (For a review of how faulty thinking develops refer to the chapter on self-image.)

To best describe the thinking process of a depressed individual let us consider three faulty patterns of thought which distort the individual's total view of life. We will call this pattern the *Depressive Triad.*

The first part of the Depressive Triad is concerned with a person looking at his experiences in a negative manner. This gives him a negative view of the world. He interprets (whether right or wrong) his interactions with the world as representing defeat, disparagement, or deprivation. All of life is filled with burdens and obstacles and these detract from the person. *Negative thinking can lead a person into depression. And when he is depressed he continues to think more and more negatively, which reinforces the depression.*

The person with a negative view of the world interprets his experiences as actually detracting from him-

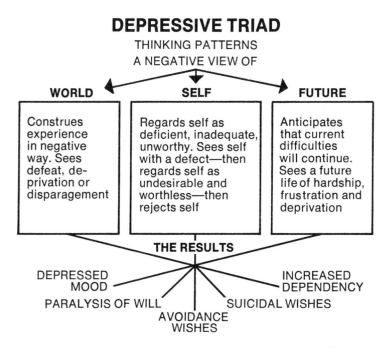

DEPRESSIVE TRIAD

THINKING PATTERNS
A NEGATIVE VIEW OF

WORLD	SELF	FUTURE
Construes experience in negative way. Sees defeat, deprivation or disparagement	Regards self as deficient, inadequate, unworthy. Sees self with a defect—then regards self as undesirable and worthless—then rejects self	Anticipates that current difficulties will continue. Sees a future life of hardship, frustration and deprivation

THE RESULTS

DEPRESSED MOOD   INCREASED DEPENDENCY

PARALYSIS OF WILL   SUICIDAL WISHES

AVOIDANCE WISHES

self. Even neutral experiences are interpreted in a negative manner. A neutral attitude on the part of a friend is seen as rejection. A neutral comment is interpreted as a hostile remark. His thinking pattern is clouded by reading into the remarks of others that which fits his previously drawn negative conclusions. He makes assumptions and selective abstractions, generalizes, and magnifies events and remarks way out of proportion. He is so predisposed to negative thinking that he automatically makes negative interpretations of situations. Defeat is his byword.

A depression-prone teacher was given a new responsibility in his department. His immediate reaction was, "I'll never be able to do this." A new goal or task was an impossibility to him. Looking in his briefcase for a pen he knew he had put there that morning, he began to think, "I'll never find this." He had only been looking for three seconds. Any kind of problem was overwhelming. Upon returning home he discovered that a dog had rummaged through the garbage cans and distributed the mess all over the driveway. The teacher's reaction was that the mess was too much to clean up. He couldn't possibly do it by himself and so he left it. He was not lazy—he actually felt that way. People with this type of depression are capable of doing the job but they underestimate themselves. Even if they are able to accomplish most of what they do, they view themselves as a *total failure.*

Deprivation is another common reaction. The depressed person interprets a minor event as being a great loss. A young man pulled into the parking lot at church on his way to see his pastor. Just as he pulled in, another car got in his way and stalled for twenty seconds. His first thought was, "I am losing valuable time which can never be made up." He went into the office and had to sit there waiting alone for ten minutes. Again he was disturbed because no one else was in the office and he was missing the companionship of other people.

Such feelings can also center around the loss of money. The person interprets the spending of money for legitimate things as a loss, even spending twenty cents to ride the bus or paying a dime for a phone call.

Self-depreciation is another common way of thinking that leads to depression. The person is hypersensitive to the reactions of other people. Someone may make a neutral (or even kind) remark, but he takes it as ridicule or an insult. A favorable comment is misinterpreted and if a person does not speak to him he feels totally rejected. (Remember the earlier example of the woman whose pastor did not speak to her as she left church.)

A certain young woman had a straight A average the first two years of college. But whenever other students were asked for their comments in class she would think, "Why didn't the teacher call on me? He must think I don't have the answer and that I'm dumb!" If a self-depreciating person was standing in line to enter a theater and someone crowded in front, he would think, "That person thinks I'm the sort he can do that to and get away with it."

The impossible manner in which the person views himself leaves no way out for him. A young man, sitting in a class where he rarely spoke, thought, "I bet they think I'm stupid because I don't say anything." When he did speak he thought, "They must think I talk too much." No matter what he does he downgrades himself.

These situations illustrate the next major characteristic of the depressed person's thinking. He has a negative view of himself. He constantly devalues himself regardless of circumstances or events.

The normal person takes one shortcoming or setback in stride but the depressed person generalizes. To him one setback means that he is a total failure and unacceptable. When a young fellow asked a girl for a date she said no because of prior commitments. But he generalized and thought, "Boy, I must be unacceptable to girls." A man who invested in the stock market made money on nine transactions but lost some on the tenth. He generalized and thought, "I'm a terrible businessman. I'm really dumb."

This negative thinking grows so out of proportion that it is the main characteristic of the person's self-concept. And he associates the negative thinking with self-rejection. Not only does he view himself as inferior but he dislikes himself for it! If he knows that he is depressed, instead of trying to do something about it he criticizes himself for being that way. The main point to remember is that when the depressed person sees problems of rejection, or experiences setbacks, he does not blame others. He blames himself.

How does negative thinking develop in a person? In the chapter on self-image we discuss the development of one's self-concept. This image can contribute to a predisposition toward depression if the person's thinking pattern is basically negative. As the person grows and develops he begins to interpret experiences as personal defeats. He believes these defeats occur because of some defect within himself. Because he has this defect he thinks of himself as a worthless person. He even blames himself for having developed this defective trait and views himself with distaste. Because this trait is part of him he sees no hope of ever changing. Thus the future seems dismal.

A person with this mental attitude is very prone to depression. Much of his depression is simply due to a faulty thought pattern. He has been sensitized to certain types of life situations and any stresses which are similar may precipitate depression. Any situation that lowers the individual's self-esteem brings on depression, such as failing an exam, being rejected, or being blocked from achieving an important goal. A successful salesman was asked to go to the opposite side of the country to head up a new branch office at double his salary. But to do so he would have to leave the girl he was seriously courting. This was the first girl who had really responded to him, but he wanted to make sure of the relationship so that if they married the marriage would last. His parents had been divorced three times. He viewed the conflict as unsolvable and felt hopeless.

Another person discovered a lump in his arm. In spite of repeated tests and reassurances from physicians he became more and more convinced that he had developed incurable cancer. He felt there was no hope for the future.

Aaron T. Beck illustrates further:

A successful businessman stated that he had always felt inferior to his classmates who came from prosperous families because he was from a poor family. He always felt distinctly different and unacceptable. When, as an adult, he was with people wealthier than he, this caused him to have thoughts that he did not belong, that he wasn't as good as the others, and that he was a social outcast. These ideas were associated with transient feelings of sadness. At one point in his career, he was elected to the board of directors of a corporation. He viewed the other directors as coming from the "right side of the tracks" and himself as from "the wrong side." He felt he could not measure up to the other directors and slipped into a depression lasting several days.

Each of these situations would have been less of a problem had the individual not had some prior conditioning and been predisposed to reacting in a negative manner. A nondepressive person or one with a healthy self-image would still be able to function and would not be bound by reverses.

A negative view of the future is the final main pattern. "No hope!" is the cry. If I am a failure now, if I am suffering reverses and rejections now, that's the way things will be forever! The current situation has no time limit and will continue. He sees a future life of the same. The near future and the far future are both in this frame of thinking. The depressed person awakens in the morning and thinks the day is going to be lousy. He thinks of the errands he has to make downtown and feels sure he won't be able to accomplish them. He will probably get lost or back the car into someone!

This negative view of the future is different from fear. The anxious person is worried about the possibility of these things happening. But the depressed individual is *certain* these events will happen. They represent the futility of the future ever changing and the uselessness of even trying. He is resigned to the fact that this is just the continuation of what has been and ever will continue in his life.

Refer back to the chart of the Depressive Triad and you can see the final results of these three patterns of thinking. The depressed mood comes directly from the thought pattern. The normal person may feel bad if he is rejected by someone. But the depressed person feels bad simply by *thinking* he was rejected even if he wasn't. The main point to remember is that a depressive person's reaction is based upon a faulty interpretation of the available information rather than on incorrect information! Once this depressive machinery is in operation the pattern builds and builds and builds. And what is so difficult is that a new viewpoint or a proper interpretation is subjected to the same distorting process.

In addition to the depressed mood, paralysis of the will, avoidance wishes, suicidal thoughts and increasing dependencies intensify. The depressed person immobilizes himself and may not want to see friends, go to work, or even out of the house.

Wanting others to do things for him or feeling that he cannot accomplish much himself forces him to become dependent. The final stage and the most tragic is that of suicide. Not all depressives are suicidal nor are all those who commit suicide depressed. But the two often go hand in hand. Leonard Cammer in *Up From Depression* offers suggestions on what to say to a depressed person.

Jonah cried out to God that he wanted to die. So did Elijah when he fled from Jezebel. Most people experience depression to one degree or another at some time during their lifetime. And we all think negatively at times. But serious consequences will result if a person allows negative thinking to become a pattern for his life. Positive thinking leads to better emotional reactions and a stable life.

The Reversal

How do we get rid of depression? The first step is to *rule out any physical reason,* which means having a complete examination by a physician. Consider your sleeping and eating habits. If none of these is the cause, ask yourself: What am I doing that is causing me to be depressed? How and about what am I thinking that could be making me depressed?

Severe depression brought on by improper self-concepts and thought patterns may require therapy and, for some, hospitalization. If a person is depressed he should always seek assistance from someone, whether it be a physician, a qualified pastor, or a counselor.

Many people who experience depression periodically or continuously could reverse the process by restructuring their thought pattern. The first step is to *recognize and identify the thoughts that you express to yourself.* (At this point it may be helpful to reread the chapter on thoughts and feelings.) When an event occurs and a person experiences depression, he fails to realize that there is more than just this particular stimulus and response. Between the two there is a thought or a value judgment that he is making about himself, whom he views as the real culprit. Perhaps this was one of the characteristics of the type of imagination God reacted against in Genesis 6:5 AMPLIFIED where we read, *The Lord saw that the wickedness of man was great in the earth, and that every imagination and intention of all human thinking was only evil continually.*

A woman drops a dish, breaks it and feels depressed. Between the act and the depression was the thought, "I am so clumsy. I cannot be trusted even to pick up a dish." It was that type of thinking that elicited the depression. The more you identify your thoughts the more you can question and determine the validity of the thought. You may discover a pattern to these thoughts—a negative view of yourself, deprivation, or a false view of the future.

A second step is to *realize that many of these thoughts are automatic.* Sometimes we put these thoughts into our minds but in many cases they are involuntary. The severely depressed person is invaded by these thoughts and has little resistance to them. But for the person who is less ill it is possible to recognize that these thoughts are involuntary and they are *not the result of deliberation or reasoning.* They are almost an obsession. By reasoning and consideration the rational thinking process *can* overrule and put events into the proper perspective. A detachment toward our thoughts will help in transforming them.

A third step is to **distinguish between ideas and facts.** Simply because a person thinks something does not make it true nor does it mean that he should believe it. A person's thoughts do not always represent reality and they should be validated before they are accepted. A high-school girl thought her girl friends no longer liked or accepted her. Before accepting this as true, however, she was told to check out her observations and consider other reasons for the reaction of the girl friends. She also considered other hypotheses to account for the apparent situation and learned how to view the events differently. By doing this she found out that her initial thoughts were invalid.

But what if she had found them to be valid? What then? At that point she might again cloud her thinking by degrading herself and believing that the situation would never change. Instead she should investigate the reasons for the rejection, attempt to correct and rectify the problem, and discover new girl friends. She should also realize that all of us experience rejection, whether right or wrong, from time to time. But life does not come to a halt because of it. An important part of the process involves checking the accuracy and thoroughness of our first observations. Jumping to conclusions and first impressions are not always accurate. They need to be questioned.

The fourth step is often difficult but is very important. **After discovering that a particular thought is** *not true, state precisely why it is inaccurate or invalid.* Putting the reasons into words helps in three ways. It reduces the frequency of the ideas coming back again, the intensity of the idea is decreased, and finally, the feeling or mood that the idea generates is lessened.

To help even more it is important to identify specifically the kind of faulty thinking you engage in. Generalizations? Do you magnify the problem? Jump to conclusions? Learn to say, "Hey, I'm jumping to a conclusion again," or, "I exaggerated again. That isn't true." Strange as it seems, it is important for the person (when he is alone) to say this aloud and hear his own voice expressing it.

Another method is to consider alternative explanations to the events. Did you interpret the situation correctly or could there be another explanation? Remember the situation of the woman who was not greeted by the pastor at the door? As she considered an alternate explanation the situation was brought into a more realistic perspective.

Some people become depressed because they concentrate upon failures, losses, or difficulties in the past. By concentrating on them they allow themselves to be controlled and limited by the past. But to be miserable now because of something that occurred (or so you thought) in the past does not make sense. It is really a waste of energy that could be directed toward some constructive action.

Another problem of letting the past depress us is the failure and inactivity it imposes upon us for the present. "It is always wrong to mortgage the present by the past," says Martyn Lloyd-Jones, and ". . . to allow the past to act as a brake upon the present." If you are really sorry about what happened in the past and feel that things were wasted, wouldn't it be better to force yourself to move ahead now and make up for it in the future?

The example of Elijah in 1 Kings 18 and 19 vividly illustrates both the cause and the cure of one man's depression. The depression came after his triumph upon Mount Carmel and the event that triggered it was the threat of Jezebel (*see* verse 19:2). Jezebel was greatly angered by Elijah's victory and threatened him with the same fate to which he had subjected the prophets of Baal. Many despondencies can be traced to a single action or word. The problem is not the deed or the word but the person's own subjective interpretation and reaction to it. James Vold in his article "God's Cure for Emotional Depression" depicted the results of this depression and then God's answer. The following is an adaptation.

The tortures of depression are depicted very clearly (1 Kings 19:3,4,10,14). Elijah's depressed mood caused him to leave his familiar surroundings and faithful servant. This discontent with ordinary associations and friends is the companion of depression.

Secondly, Elijah prayed for death. Disgust with life and a longing for suicide seem to accompany the gloom of despondency. Elijah wasn't the only one who felt this way.

And Moses heard the people weeping throughout their families, every man at the door of his tent; and the anger of the Lord blazed hotly, and in the eyes of Moses it was evil. And Moses said to the Lord, Why have You dealt ill with Your servants? And why have

I not found favor in Your sight, that You lay the burden
of all this people on me? Have I conceived all this
people? Have I brought them forth, that You should
say to me, Carry them in your bosom, as a nursing
father carries the sucking child, to the land which You
swore to their fathers [to give them]? Where should I
get meat to give to all these people? For they weep
before me and say, Give us meat, that we may eat. I
am not able to carry all these people alone, because
the burden is too heavy for me. And if this is the way
You deal with me, kill me, I pray You, at once and be
granting me a favor, and let me not see my wretched-
ness [in the failure of all my efforts].

Numbers 11:10–15 AMPLIFIED

Moses complained to God, "Why me? Why do I have
to have this burden?" He also felt that he was carrying
around the entire burden himself (verse 14). His feelings of inferiority are also revealed (verse 15). Many
people who feel inferior are reluctant to relinquish
their authority or tasks to others and yet the amount of
work they must do is overwhelming. God gave a very
simple answer. He divided up the labor by appointing
seventy men of the elders of Israel. This is an important
lesson for us to learn—to allow others to help and to
face our inferiority feelings and deal with them realistically.

Elijah reached the depths of depression when he
started to argue with God. This action reveals another
effect of depression. It causes a loss of personal confidence in the promises of God. This lack of confidence
in God is often accompanied by the belief that God
is considered both unwise and unfair. Elijah was not
flippant or sarcastic in his conversation with God.

He was very perplexed.

Fourth, Elijah thought of himself as alone. He suffered from what men call megalomania, "an excessive concept of one's own importance." Depression shrinks one's outlook until life is limited to self. A person is persuaded that the whole world is against him. This view leads to self-pity with a total loss of perspective.

There were many ways in which God ministered to Elijah and his depression. The first phase of treatment was physical. Elijah asked for death (1 Kings 19:4) but God gave him the essentials of life (verse 6). Bread and water were delivered by an angel. The provision here was a proper diet and sufficient sleep. Proper food and rest are essential to psychological and physical health. Many problems have seemed less insoluble after a sleep. Any individual with a tendency to emotional exhaustion needs to guard against excessive weariness and improper eating habits.

The second aspect of the treatment for Elijah was psychological and spiritual. Elijah was given the opportunity to "get everything off his chest." Elijah's reply to God's question of "Why are you here?" was simple. "I am despondent and have in a sense deserted my post of duty . . . (another accomplice of depression, the resignation from responsibility) because I have been zealous for God and forsaken by Him. I am all alone and my life is in danger because of my faithfulness" (*see* 1 Kings 19:10). These words express a question as to God's dealings with him; they presuppose total loneliness and they also attribute to the people of Israel a murderous desire on their part.

God did not forsake him and He showed Elijah that Israel wasn't trying to kill him. Jezebel was the only one. There were seven thousand others who were faithful, too. God, in His time, answered Elijah and showed him that his confession was not accurate. Elijah is a good example of a person who misinterprets a situation and sees only certain elements of it. He made misconceptions concerning himself, others, and God. This in itself was enough to bring on the depression. It can bring on depression for us, too! God revealed to Elijah His purpose, and this explanation helped him to regain the proper perspective. Often our perspective is changed by opening ourselves to God and His plans.

If you are depressed, ask yourself these questions and apply to each the principles discussed in this chapter.

1. What are your eating and sleeping habits?
2. When was the last time you had a complete physical exam by a physician?
3. Are you taking any medications or drugs which might be building up in your system?
4. Do you have any disease or illness at the present time which might contribute to depression?
5. Have you evaluated the kind of depression you have, based on the information you have just read?
6. Have you evaluated your pattern of thinking as suggested in this chapter and the chapter on your thought-life?
7. Are you following your normal routine of life or are you withdrawing by staying in bed longer, staying away from your friends, avoiding regular activities? If so, it is important to force yourself to stay active while following the other principles suggested for dealing with depression.
8. Do you spend time studying and reflecting upon the Word of God? Do you have a consistent time of talking and listening to God?

The Cross of Jesus Christ offers hope to the depressed.

The Lord is my light and my salvation; whom shall I fear *or* dread? The Lord is the refuge *and* stronghold of my life; of whom shall I be afraid? When the wicked, even my enemies and my foes, came upon me to eat up my flesh, they stumbled and fell. Though a host encamp against me, my heart shall not fear; though war arise against me, (even then) in this will I be confident.

Psalms 27:1–3 AMPLIFIED

For the rest, brethren, whatever is true, whatever is worthy of reverence *and* is honorable *and* seemly, whatever is just, whatever is pure, whatever is lovely *and* lovable, whatever is kind *and* winsome *and* gracious, if there is any virtue *and* excellence, if there is anything worthy of praise, think on *and* weigh and take account of these things—fix your minds on them.

Philippians 4:8 AMPLIFIED

6
Make the Most of Your Anger

I was angry with my friend;
My friend died.
My dead anger has decayed before me.
It reeks and sickens me.
I cannot escape from its bitter stench.

AUTHOR UNKNOWN

You have just spent several hours cleaning your home and in less than five minutes the kids make a shambles of it. You feel frustrated and soon this frustration turns to anger—your pulse rate accelerates and your breathing becomes deeper and more rapid, your voice is sharp and rises in pitch as you scream at the kids to clean up the mess they've made. You want to strike back at those who have created so much work for you. Your reactions are driven by the increased adrenalin that is surging into your bloodstream. You are not having a heart attack or a breakdown—but just experiencing anger. You may get angry occasionally, once or twice a week, or several times a day. But, like every other person who has ever lived upon this earth, at some time you will get angry.

Anger is a *strong emotion of displeasure.* When it is present it produces energy in abundance. It impels individuals to do things that tend to hurt or destroy. Some of the many names for anger are aggression, resentment, frustration, hate, fury, indignation, outrage, wrath, antagonism, crossness, hostility, bitterness, destructiveness, spite, rancor, ferocity, scorn, disdain, enmity, malevolence, and defiance. When a person is angry we say he is mad, bitter, frustrated, griped, fed up, sore, excited, seething, annoyed, troubled, antagonistic, exasperated, vexed, indignant, furious, provoked, hurt, irked, irritated, sick, pained, cross, hostile, ferocious, savage, vicious, deadly, dangerous, or offensive. Anger motivates a person to hate, wound, damage, annihilate, despise, scorn, disdain, loathe, vilify, curse, despoil, ruin, demolish, abhor, abominate, desolate, ridicule, tease, kid, get even, laugh at, humiliate, goad, shame, criticize, scold, bawl out, irritate, beat up, fight, compete with, crush, offend, or bully. A person is considered angry when he attacks other people verbally or subtly.

What happens to your body when you get angry? Many physical changes occur (*see* Diagram). The body prepares for action. Sugar pours into the system, creating energy. Your blood pressure increases, heart beats faster, and blood containing needed nourishment circulates more rapidly through your body. Your blood clots much more quickly than normal. This serves a useful purpose for if you are injured while you are angry the clotting action will help stop the bleeding. Additional adrenalin is released, which dilates the pupils of your eyes and makes you see better and mobilizes you for action. Your muscles tense up—in fact, the muscles at the outlet of the stomach squeeze down so tightly that nothing can leave your stomach while you are angry. The digestive tract can become so spastic that severe abdominal pains are felt during or after the time you are angry.

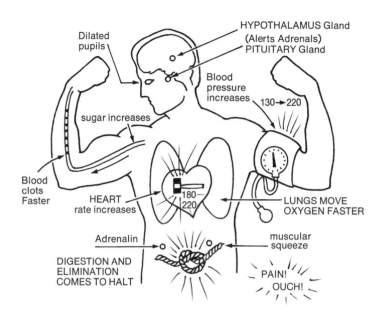

Your blood pressure may increase from 130 to 230 and your heart beats faster—often up to 220 or higher. People have had strokes during a fit of anger because of the increased blood pressure. During anger the arteries of the heart can squeeze down hard enough to produce angina pectoris or even a fatal coronary attack.

What happens if your anger is not released? Your body remains ready for action with your heart beating rapidly, blood pressure up, and blood chemical changes taking place. The results can be physically harmful.

Look at the result of anger in the life of Nabal (*see* 1 Samuel 25). David sent some of his men to Nabal who was very wealthy. They wanted some food, but instead Nabal gave them a rebuke and sent them away. David upon hearing this gathered his men together and set out to fight Nabal. But Abigail, Nabal's wife, heard what her husband had done, and gathering together a large store of food went out, met David and his men and appeased them by her gift of food.

> And Abigail came to Nabal; and behold, he was holding a feast in his house, like the feast of a king; and *his* heart was merry, for he was very drunk; so she told him nothing at all until the morning light. But in the morning, when the wine was gone out of Nabal, and his wife told him these things, his heart died within him, and he became [paralyzed, helpless as] a stone. And about ten days after that, the Lord smote Nabal and he died.
>
> 1 Samuel 25:36,37 AMPLIFIED

The phrase *his heart died within him* in the original could mean he had a stroke or a heart attack. Why did this happen? How would Nabal react to his wife's disclosure? Probably intense anger can bring about such a physical response!

Why do we become angry? Are there logical reasons for anger?

Some people become angry when they are *frustrated.* When a person is blocked from obtaining satisfaction or fulfilling his desires, impulses, ambitions, hopes, or drives, he becomes angry. An individual ignores your requests or an employee at work continually blocks your efforts for promotion. The result? Anger. "Why doesn't he do what I want, or get out of my way?" Anger can also be directed toward ourselves when we discover the part we play in contributing to our own frustration.

A person may get angry when he is *experiencing pain*

—either physical or psychological. A child who is being spanked may suddenly turn to his parents and cry, "I hate you!" Harsh or brutal words or experiences that hurt can also make us angry. *How long will you vex and torment me and break me in pieces with words?* Job cried out to his friends (Job 19:2 AMPLIFIED).

Another reason for anger is *anxiety*, over a threat to oneself or a possession, or a loss. But the anxiety so quickly turns into anger. We choose anger because as Harry Stack Sullivan in *The Psychiatric Interview* observed:

Anger is much more pleasant to experience than anxiety. The brute facts are that it is much more comfortable to feel angry than anxious. Admitting that neither is too delightful, there is everything in favor of anger. Anger often leaves one sort of worn out . . . and very often makes things worse in the long run, but there is a curious feeling of power when one is angry.

Injustice is another cause of anger. Injustices occur every day and are perpetrated upon people in all levels of society. Yet we often lack the initiative to react to injustices inflicted upon people who are not on our own level. Far too little anger is expressed over the injustices many people suffer, yet it is perhaps one of the most valid reasons for anger.

A final cause of anger is *selfishness*. We want our own way regardless of what happens to others. Some of our frustrations could easily be traced to the fact that our way has been blocked. We could give in and let the other person have his way, thus eliminating the anger. But instead we become frustrated and angry. A subtle expression of this selfishness is criticism of others. We become angry because other people fail to meet the unrealistic expectations we have of them. Though we are not perfect we expect other people to be. Perhaps it is the awareness of our own imperfections that leads us to attack and become angry with those who fail to live up to our expectations. If the anger were directed toward ourselves it would be difficult to handle and unacceptable. Instead, we criticize others which makes us feel better at their expense. In *Psychology and Morals* Dr. James Hadfield suggests:

It is literally true that in judging others we are trumpeting abroad our own secret faults. We personalize our unrecognized failings, and hate in others the sins to which we are secretly addicted.

He goes on to say that the real reason for our condemnation of certain sins in others is that these same sins are a temptation to us. It is for this very reason that we denounce so vehemently the miserliness, bigotry, or cynicism of others. Whatever fault we least tolerate in others is likely to be amongst our own besetting sins.

Most of our emotions are directed against ourselves. . . . Allow any man to give free vent to his feelings and then you may, with perfect safety, turn and say: "Thou art the man."

What makes *you* get angry? Perhaps the reasons vary. The next time you start to get angry, you might do well to ask yourself, "Is this really worth getting all this upset over?"

It is obvious that anger is here to stay and all of us will experience it. But as Christians we must ask some further questions. Is anger right or wrong? How do we deal with anger? Can it be controlled? When is it right to be angry? Is it ever wrong *not* to be angry with someone or a situation?

The Bible gives many examples of individuals who were angry and also indicates whether the results of that anger were positive or negative. Take for example the story of Cain and Abel—the first biblical instance of anger.

> But for Cain and his offering He had no respect *or* regard. So Cain was exceedingly angry *and* indignant, and he looked sad *and* depressed. And the Lord said to Cain, Why are you angry?
>
> Genesis 4:5,6 AMPLIFIED

Cain was angry with his brother because Abel's sacrifice was accepted and Cain's was not. First Cain experiences anger in his heart, then it shows on his face and then the action of anger is recorded (*see* verse 4:8). Anger usually has some result. In this situation the anger culminated in murder—Cain kills his brother Abel. Cain is alienated from his brother, from God and from others. Anger can also result in loneliness—an angry man may be the loneliest of men.

Another biblical character who experienced anger was Moses. Returning from the mountain after receiving the Ten Commandments from God, Moses encountered a strange situation in the Israelite camp.

> And as soon as he came near to the camp he saw the calf and the dancing. And Moses' anger blazed hot, and he cast the tables out of his hands, and broke them at the foot of the mountain. And he took the calf they had made, and burned it in the fire, and ground it to

powder, and scattered it on the water, and made the
Israelites drink it.

Exodus 32:19, 20 AMPLIFIED

While Moses had been in the presence of God the
people had constructed their own idol out of gold.
Moses was so angry over their deed he cracked the
tablets of stone on which the Ten Commandments had
been inscribed. Was Moses right in his outburst of anger? Was this not a destructive act? Might it not have
been better for him to have reasoned with the people
and preserved the tablets?

Saul's anger toward David and Jonathan is another
illustration of the destructive force of anger.

And the women responded, as they laughed *and* fro-
licked, saying Saul has slain his thousands, and David
his ten thousands. And Saul was very angry, for the
saying displeased him.

1 Samuel 18:7,8 AMPLIFIED

Jealousy and envy toward David progressed to anger
and hatred, and not far behind was action—attempts to
take David's life. Later Saul's anger turned toward his
own son.

Then Saul's anger was kindled against Jonathan, and
he said to him, You son of a perverse, rebellious
woman, do not I know that you have chosen the son
of Jesse to your shame, and to the shame of your
mother who bore you? But Saul cast his spear at him
to smite him, by which Jonathan knew that his father
had determined to kill David.

1 Samuel 20:30, 33 AMPLIFIED

Here is a clear example of how anger can be overly destructive, even against one's own family. When a person allows himself to be governed by emotion instead of fact, he may impulsively react in ways that are decidedly destructive. Each year in the United States thousands of children are classified in the "battered child" category because a parent's anger got out of control. Many parents and spouses live with overwhelming regrets because of actions made in anger toward other family members.

In the same account of Saul and Jonathan another instance of anger is recorded. This time it is Jonathan who is angry.

> So Jonathan arose from the table in fierce anger and ate no food that second day of the month, for he grieved for David, because his father had disgraced him.
>
> 1 Samuel 20:34 AMPLIFIED

His anger was intense because of his father's actions and attempts upon David's life. Saul had violated a basic principle of parenthood which was later expressed in the New Testament: *Fathers, do not provoke your children to anger* (*see* Ephesians 6:4). When a parent provokes his child, the offspring has reason to be angry. In this particular situation anger was a healthy reaction. But notice the difference in the resulting reaction. Jonathan simply did not eat (which was probably best for his stomach at that moment!) and he went away. His action was not destructive. He did not attempt to argue or strike back. He simply left the area of the protagonist and source of his anger.

Still another example is that of Jonah whose anger led

him to depression and suicidal thoughts. We learn *But it displeased Jonah exceedingly, and he was very angry.* He was angry, believe it or not, because the people of Nineveh had turned away from their sins and God had forgiven them and had mercy upon them! In utter despair Jonah asked God to take his life. God responded by asking Jonah *Do you do well to be angry?* The first time Jonah was quiet and did not answer God. Later on Jonah again asked God to let him die. *And God said to Jonah, Do you do well to be angry for the loss of the gourd? And he said, I do well to be angry, angry enough to die!* (*See* Jonah 4 AMPLIFIED.)

At this point Jonah was not using his faculty of reason. An angry man usually does not make rational decisions. Jonah had experienced a terrific storm at sea and survived the episode with the great fish. Yet because God had apparently changed his mind about the impending judgment of Nineveh, Jonah became angry and his anger led to depression and self-pity. It was impossible to reason with him. He simply wanted to die. Many people channel their anger back toward themselves in this manner. They become depressed and actually take out their frustrations upon themselves.

Jesus Christ experienced anger in His life, and for a very good reason. Norman V. Hope in "How to Be Good and Mad" gives some examples.

The gospel records make it perfectly plain that he could on occasion feel blazing anger and, feeling it, could and did give emphatic expression to it. For example, in Mark, chapter 3, the story is told of his healing on the Sabbath a man with a withered hand. When some protested that it was altogether improper to heal a man on the Sabbath, Jesus was indignant at their stubbornly perverted sense of values. The Scripture says that he "looked round about on them with anger, being grieved for the hardness of their hearts." In Matthew 23, the account is given of Jesus' blasting the scribes and Pharisees, whom he describes as "hypocrites" for the revolting contrast between their high religious profession and their low irreligious practices. And in John 2 it is recorded that Jesus cleansed the Temple of its money-changers, insisting that his Father's house must not be made a house of merchandise.

Jesus felt free to be angry and to let it show and to express it clearly.

It should be obvious from these illustrations that anger is not necessarily bad. But the results of anger can be either constructive or destructive, positive or negative.

Anger is a force, a gunpowder which, depending upon how it is directed, can blast away at wrong or can be used for wrong itself.

When used constructively, anger can sometimes help us accomplish great feats of strength. A person who is angry enough may be able to lift something which he would not otherwise be able to handle, such as raising a car off a loved one who is trapped underneath. Leo Madow tells the story in *Anger—How to Recognize and Cope With It* of a woman whose anger actually helped her function better.

She had been called as a witness in a trial and was terrified at the prospect of being interrogated. Before she was called to the witness stand she described her brain as being a "sack of mush" and she was not sure she would be able to remember her own name. Meanwhile the witness ahead of her in the case was saying things which were not true. As the woman listened to the testimony she became angrier and angrier. When she went on the stand her mind was as sharp as a steel trap. She was able to testify very accurately, recalled many details that she was not aware she had known, and made a most effective witness. As she explained afterward, she became so angry at the lies of the previous witness that she forgot all her fears. It is worth noting that an extremely effective means of utilizing anger is in overcoming fear.

Constructively used, anger can give strength both physically and mentally. Such normal outlets for anger are dependent on several factors. First, the individual must not be overwhelmed by his anger, because he is then rendered ineffective. Second, there should not be so much fear of anger that it cannot be released directly, as it will then come out in unhealthy ways. Third, opportunities for some socially acceptable outlet must exist.

Ephesians 4:24 tells us to *Be angry and sin not.* The word *angry* in this verse means an anger which is an abiding and settled habit of the mind, and which is aroused under certain conditions. The person is aware and in control of it. There is a just occasion for the anger here. Reason is involved and when reason is present anger such as this is right. The Scriptures not only permit it but on some occasions **demand it!** Perhaps this sounds strange to some who have thought for years that anger is all wrong. But the Word of God states that we **are to be angry!** as explained by Spiros Zodhiates in *The Pursuit of Happiness.*

This, then, immediately disposes of the idea that the meek are passive persons who never get angry. There is no passivity in meekness. When the Lord Jesus Christ comes into our hearts, He does not go to sleep and put us to sleep. He becomes aggressively active within us.

. . . a Christian does and should get angry. But he must be careful to get angry at the right things and refrain from getting angry at the wrong things. Before he was saved and became blessed, his anger was sinful. Now it must be righteous. Meekness is the sanctification of anger. It includes patience and long-suffering for personal affronts, with the willingness to speak out vigorously in defense of the Gospel. To get angry at what we should and when we should is a definitely Christian characteristic.

As Dr. J. H. Jowett says, "A life incapable of anger is destitute of the needful energy for all reform. There is no blaze in it, there is no ministry of purification. If a city is to be purged from its filth it will have to be by souls that are burning with moral resentment. It is the man who is 'fervent in spirit' who will most assuredly 'serve the Lord.' 'The grass withereth . . . because the spirit of the Lord breatheth upon it.' The Church needs more of this withering breath and consuming energy that is born of holy wrath against all established wrong. We are taught in the New Testament that this power of indignation is begotten by the Holy Spirit. The Holy Spirit makes us capable of healthy heat, and it inspires the fire within us. The Holy Spirit never creates a character that is lukewarm, neutral, or indifferent."

Righteous anger is not sinful when it is properly directed. Such anger is an abiding settled attitude of righteous indignation against sin, coupled with appropriate action.

There are several characteristics of righteous anger. First of all it must be controlled, not a heated, nor unrestrained passion. Even if the cause is legitimate and is directed at an injustice, uncontrolled anger can cause great error in judgment and increase the difficulty. The mind must be in control of the emotions so that the ability to reason is not lost. *Be angry and sin not.*

Second, there must be no hatred, malice, or resentment. Anger that harbors a counterattack only complicates the problem. Jesus' reaction to the injustices delivered against Him is a good example.

> When he was reviled *and* insulted, He did not revile *or* offer insult in return; when He was abused *and* suffered, He made no threats [of vengeance]; but He trusted [Himself and everything] to Him Who judges fairly.
>
> 1 Peter 2:23 AMPLIFIED

> Beloved, never avenge yourselves, but leave the way open for [God's] wrath; for it is written, Vengeance is Mine, I will repay . . . says the Lord.
>
> Romans 12:19 AMPLIFIED

A third characteristic of righteous anger is that its motivation is unselfish. When the motivation is selfish, usually pride and resentment are involved. Anger should be directed not at the wrong done to oneself but at injustice done to others. Upon seeing the slave market for the first time, Abraham Lincoln is said to have vowed to hit that problem someday—and hit it hard. Years later he issued the Emancipation Proclamation.

Florence Nightingale was known for her anger against the evils of the day which she encountered in the hospitals. Although she was a small woman, strong men feared her presence because her anger was directed with determined stubbornness, which eventually led to reforms.

Similarly, Norman Hope relates a case of unselfish anger.

The incident that inspired the career of the great English philanthropist Lord Shaftesbury took place when he was about fourteen. One day he was startled to hear a great shouting and yelling in a side street and the singing of a bacchanalian song. Presently the noisy party neared the corner, and to his horror he saw four or five drunken men carrying a roughly made coffin containing the body of one of their fellows. Staggering as they turned the corner, they let their burden fall and then broke out into foul language. The horrified young boy stood spellbound as the bizarre funeral procession passed. Then he exclaimed, "Good heavens! Can this be permitted, simply because the man was poor and friendless?" Before the sound of the drunken songs had died away in the distance, he had determined that, with the help of God, he would from that time on devote his life to pleading the cause of the poor and friendless.

Another characteristic of righteous anger is that it is directed against wrong deeds or situations, not against people. Jesus said that we are to love all people. He excludes no one. We can hate the sin and be angry at it, but we must love the sinner. This is difficult for some people to grasp. It seems like a paradox to say that we can love a sinner and yet hate his actions or sin. Some say this is impossible. After struggling with this question for a long time, C. S. Lewis eventually came to a most articulate solution, as related in *Mere Christianity*.

For a long time I used to think this a silly, straw-splitting distinction: how could you hate what a man did and not hate the man? But years later it occurred to me that there was one man to whom I had been doing this all my life—namely myself. However much I might dislike my own cowardice or conceit or greed, I went on loving myself. There had never been the slightest difficulty about it. In fact the very reason why I hated the things was that I loved the man. Just because I loved myself, I was sorry to find that I was the sort of man who did those things. Consequently, Christianity does not want us to reduce by one atom the hatred we feel for cruelty and treachery. We ought to hate them. . . . But it does want us to hate them in the same way in which we hate things in ourselves; being sorry that the man should have done such things, and hoping, if it is anyway possible, that somehow, sometime, somewhere, he can be cured and made human again.

Our anger must be directed toward the evil a person does, but not toward the person himself.

The final characteristic of righteous anger, and the element so often lacking, is that our anger ought to lead to positive and constructive action to right the wrong. Jesus was angry at conditions about him and yet he continued to heal and preach. Shaftesbury, Lincoln, Nightingale and others directed the energy of their anger toward correcting the evils about them.

What can we do to counteract the destructive results of anger? We see a child being mistreated severely in the home next to us. Do we ignore it, just pray about it, or try to help the parent stop mistreating his child? How often do we read about children suffering in an inner-city ghetto and not feel any twinge of emotion? What about a marriage situation where the wife allows her mother to interfere in the marriage and it is obvious the couple is headed for divorce? Our failure to confront the mother is based upon the excuse, "She won't change," or "I do not want to hurt her." We are not supposed to be busybodies, but if we *could* help a person and refuse to do so, we actually contribute to the problem by not taking action.

When a problem develops, some people say, "It's not my fault, it's *his* fault. It's up to him to take the first step toward reconciliation." But Jesus said:

> So if, when you are offering your gift at the altar you there remember that your brother has any [grievance] against you, Leave your gift at the altar and go; first make peace with your brother, and then come back *and* present your gift.
>
> Matthew 5:23,24 AMPLIFIED

Regardless of who is at fault we can take the first step. Sometimes we are more involved with smaller evils than large ones. We cannot ignore either! Righteous anger, according to Hope, "not only protests but also proposes, not only raises its voice to object but also raises its hand to remedy." He illustrates by quoting A. Powell Davis:

> That is one of the truly serious things that has happened to the multitude of so-called ordinary people. They have forgotten how to be indignant. This is not because they are overflowing with human kindness, but because they are morally soft and compliant. When they see evil and injustice, they are pained but not revolted. They mutter and mumble, they never cry out. They commit the sin of not being angry.
>
> Yet their anger is the one thing above all others that would make them count. If they cannot lead crusades, or initiate reforms, they can at least create the conditions in which

crusades can be effectual and reforms successful. The wrath of the multitude could bring back decency and integrity into public life; it could frighten the corrupt demagogue into silence and blast the rumor-monger into oblivion. It could give honest leaders a chance to win.

Be angry and sin not might also be stated *Be angry and be right.* We are to be angry at the right time, in the right way, and against the right things.

The same Bible that tells us to be angry also tells us that there are times when we should not be angry at all. In Ephesians 4:31 we are told to *put off wrath.* This type of emotion refers to anger that boils up and soon subsides. It can be literally defined as a turbulent commotion and boiling agitation of feelings. Perhaps you have encountered people like that. We say they have a "short fuse." It doesn't take much to set them off. When the emotion hits, it is very intense and usually out of proportion to the situation. Paul, guided by God, says that we are not to have this type of anger.

Jesus said, *But I say to you that whosoever is angry with his brother shall be in danger of the judgment* (*see* Matthew 5:22). Some versions include the words *without a cause.* Martyn Lloyd-Jones in his *Studies in the Sermon on the Mount* says:

For us as Christians to feel enmity in our hearts is, according to our Lord Jesus Christ, to be guilty of something which, in the sight of God, is murder. To hate, to feel bitter, to have this unpleasant, unkind feeling of resentment towards a person without a cause is murder. Indeed, let me remind you that there are some authorities who say that this qualifying phrase "without a cause" should not be there. In some of the manuscripts it is omitted. It is impossible to decide exactly on grounds of textual criticism whether it should be included or not. But even taking it as it is, it is a tremendous demand; and if we leave out the qualifying phrase it is still more so. You should not be angry with your brother. Anger in the heart towards any human being, and especially to those who belong to the household of faith, is, according to our Lord, something that is as reprehensible in the sight of God as murder.

Another word for anger is found in Ephesians 4:26 where the advice is not to let the sun go down upon one's wrath. This refers to anger that is accompanied by irritation, exasperation and embitterment. This type of anger is to be gotten rid of quickly. It can be easily expressed in attitude, speech and behavior. Out of it can come a resentment that will hurt you more than it hurts others. Resentment carries with it the tinge of revenge—wanting to get back at another person or get even.

In Dr. S. I. McMillen's book *None of These Diseases* the story is told of a visit Dale Carnegie made to Yellowstone National Park. While observing the grizzly bears feeding, a guide told him that the grizzly bear could whip any animal in the West with the exception of the buffalo and the Kodiak bear. That very night as the people sat watching a grizzly eat, they noticed there was only one animal the grizzly would allow to eat with him—a skunk. Now the grizzly could have beaten the skunk in any fight. He resented the skunk and probably wanted to get even with him for coming into his own feeding domain. But he didn't attack the skunk. Why? Because he knew the high cost of getting even! It wouldn't be worth it. Many of us humans have not learned that important lesson. We spend long days and longer nights dwelling on our resentments, and even plotting ways to strike back, to our own detriment.

There is a price to pay for this kind of anger. It can lead to severed relationships with God and other people, even those to whom the anger is not directed. And for those who harbor these feelings the result may be strokes, heart attacks, high blood pressure, hypertension, mucous colitis, or ulcers. The question is, "Is it worth it?" Dr. McMillen explains:

When Jesus said, "Forgive seventy-times seven," He was thinking not only of our souls, but of saving our bodies from ulcerative colitis, toxic goiters, high blood pressure, and scores of other diseases. The advice of the Great Physician appears to have percolated even into the hard-boiled bulletin of a Milwaukee police department: "If selfish people try to take advantage of you, cross them off your list, but don't try to get even. When you try to get even, you hurt yourself more than you hurt the other fellow."

How then should a Christian deal with his anger? What choices are available to him? There are four basic ways to deal with anger.

The first way is to *repress* it. Don't even admit that you are angry. Ignore the presence of anger. This repression is often unconscious, but it is *not healthy!* Repressing anger is like placing a wastebasket full of paper in a closet and setting fire to it. The fire will either burn itself out *or* it could set the entire house on fire and burn it down. The energy produced by anger cannot be destroyed. It must be converted or directed into another channel.

One outlet for repressed anger is accidents. Perhaps you have met people who are *accident-prone.* Unfortunately, their accidents may involve other people as well as themselves. A man who is angry may slam a door on his own hand or someone else's. He may wash windows for his wife when he would rather be watching a game on TV and put his hand through the window. Perhaps his driving manifests his anger when he "accidentally" runs over the rose bushes.

Repressed anger can easily take its toll on your body by giving you a vicious headache. Your gastrointestinal system—that thirty-foot tube extending from the mouth to the rectum—reacts beautifully to repressed anger. You may experience difficulty in swallowing, nausea and vomiting, gastric ulcer, constipation, or diarrhea. The most common cause of ulcerative colitis is repressed anger. Repressed anger can affect the skin through pruritus, itching, and neurodermatitis. Respiratory disorders such as asthma are common effects and the role of anger in coronary thrombosis is fairly well accepted. In a newspaper report (Long Beach *Independent, Press-Telegram,* Jan. 24, 1973):

A Southland psychiatrist says that anger and unhappiness are responsible for most heart attacks.

Dr. Wallace C. Ellerbroek of Sunset Beach says that learned control of such thoughts is much more important in prevention of heart disease than is strict adherence to a low-cholesterol diet.

Dr. Ellerbroek, a program director at Metropolitan State Hospital at Norwalk, said in an exclusive interview that "miserable people have a high cholesterol but happy people do not."

"If you check coronary victims," he contends, "you'll find they were either depressed or angry before their coronary."

Cholesterol does play a role in heart disease, Dr. Ellerbroek explains, but it is bad emotions, not diet, that send cholesterol levels soaring.

For example, he likes to cite a study of Navy flight cadets. On the mornings the cadets were scheduled to fly, their cholesterol ranged from 400 to 650—extremely high. But on the mornings they didn't have to fly, their cholesterols were 140 to 165, he says—in other words, entirely normal.

Any negative emotion—anger, depression, frustration, irritation, unhappiness, the blues—is going to affect the entire body and brain adversely to some degree, he maintains.

Fishermen tell us that when a shark is hooked it uses its great strength to try and get away from the hook that is curtailing its freedom and which will eventually bring it to its death. The shark swims and lunges away from the boat, but after a while it tires and is slowly brought to the boat, gaffed, and lifted on board. But even then the shark does not quit. It thrashes about seeking to assault its attacker. Fishermen report they have actually seen the shark reach around and tear chunks of flesh out of its own body in its frustrated attempt to get back at the object which has lifted it out of the water.

Anger and hatred lead to further destruction. So does repression. Repressed anger or anger held in or turned inward often turns into depression. In one's unconscious attempt to handle the emotion, actual harm can be done to one's own body.

As David Augsburger writes in *Seventy Times Seven:*

Repressed anger hurts and keeps on hurting. If you always deal with it simply by holding it firmly in check or sweeping it under the rug, without any form of release or healing, it can produce rigidity and coldness in personality.

Even worse, hostilities pushed down into the depths of consciousness have a way of fermenting into other problems. Depression, anxiety and eventually mental breakdown.

Or repressed anger may come out indirectly in critical attitudes, scapegoating or irritableness. Often those we call "good people" who harbor hostility will do indirectly and unconsciously what "bad people" do directly and deliberately, because unreleased, buried anger colors their motive.

Many large companies dispose of their industrial waste material by pumping it into underground mines or abandoned wells. This works for a while but eventually it can pollute water systems or even burst out into the open through another channel.

"Do not talk when angry but after you have calmed down, do talk," says Dr. William Menninger in an article in *National Observer.* "Sometimes we push each other away and the problem between us festers and festers. Just as in surgery, free and adequate drainage is essential if healing is to take place."

Anger is an emotion that must be recognized. "When you repress or suppress those things which you don't want to live with," suggests John Powell in *Why Am I Afraid to Love?* "you don't really solve the problem because you don't bury the problem dead—you bury it alive." When God created us He included the capacity for emotional reactions. Recognize and accept your anger for what it is. Only then will you be in a position to use it wisely and properly.

A second way to handle anger is to *suppress* it. In this you are aware of your emotional reaction but you choose to hold it in and not let people know that you are angry. In some situations this can be healthy but eventually the anger has to be recognized and released in a healthy manner. Otherwise your storage apparatus will begin to overflow at the wrong time and the wrong place.

Sometimes a person chooses to suppress his anger when the person with whom he is angry could react back with more force. For example, an employer calls in one of his salesmen and chews him out for some inefficiency or problem. The salesman becomes angry but realizes that if he expresses his anger to his boss he might lose his job. So he suppresses his anger—until he arrives home. His wife greets him when he walks in the door and he replies with an angry snarl. This takes her by surprise and she will either react by snapping back at him or by following her husband's previous example and suppressing her anger. But then her teen-age son walks in and she vents her pent-up anger upon the unsuspecting boy. He takes out his anger on the younger brother who in turn kicks the dog who bites the cat who scratches the three-year-old who takes out her frustration by pulling off the head of her Barbie doll! This simple process of letting loose your anger on a less threatening person is called displacement. It may help you for a moment but it can set up a long-lasting chain of events that could reach back to you.

Guilt is another reason for displacing your anger. If you are furious with your mother but believe that one must not get angry with one's mother, then you may find yourself exploding at other older women. Or you may use displacement to avoid humiliating yourself. You are traveling with your wife and trying to make mileage on a particular day. You take a wrong turn and go seventy miles out of the way. You then project the blame onto your wife and accuse her of misguiding or distracting you.

Is the cause for your anger realistic? Is it reasonable? If so, then deal with the problem directly. If you have a disagreement with your boss over policy, the solution is not to go home and complain to your wife or to another employee. Talk with your boss and try to resolve the problem. If this is not practical, then you must put up with the situation and find other outlets for your anger.

If the cause for your anger is *not* realistic then the problem is within you. If you get angry with your spouse because he or she does not treat you the way your mother did, then you had better recognize first of all that your spouse is not your mother!

Suppressing anger has some merit, especially if it helps you relax, cool down and begin to act in a rational manner. The Word of God has quite a bit to say about this type of suppression.

He who is slow to anger has great understanding, but he who is hasty of spirit exposes *and* exalts his folly.

Proverbs 14:29 AMPLIFIED

A hot-tempered man stirs up strife, but he who is slow to anger appeases contention.

Proverbs 15:18 AMPLIFIED

He who is slow to anger is better than the mighty, and he who rules his *own* spirit than he who takes a city.

Proverbs 16:32 AMPLIFIED

Good sense makes a man restrain his anger, and it is his glory to overlook a transgression *or* an offense.

Proverbs 19:11 AMPLIFIED

Make no friendships with a man given to anger, and
with a wrathful man do not associate.

Proverbs 22:24 AMPLIFIED

A [self-confident] fool utters all his anger, but a wise
man keeps it back and stills it.

Proverbs 29:11 AMPLIFIED

Understand [this], my beloved brethren. Let every
man be quick to hear, (a ready listener,) slow to speak,
slow to take offense *and* to get angry.

James 1:19 AMPLIFIED

The individual who exerts self-control (and it *is* possible) will find that his anger level actually decreases. He
will not become as angry as if he were to simply cut
loose with his first reaction. A calm consideration of the
cause for the anger and the results will help you handle
the situation properly.

A third way to handle anger is to simply *express* it.
Some people think you should just cut loose with exactly how you feel no matter what or who is involved.
They feel this is healthy psychologically and necessary
in order to live a balanced life.

There are several ways to express your anger. One is
to react with violent passion, yelling, harsh words, and
tremendous emotion. This will bring results but you
may not care for those results. If you allow yourself the
freedom to react in this way, shouldn't you allow the
other person the freedom to react to you in the same
manner?

You can also express your anger by walking around
the block, digging in the garden for an hour, or beating
on a pillow. Or you might try writing down exactly how
you feel when you get angry, especially if it is difficult

even violence unless it is controlled by love.

3. Be angry, but only to be kind. Only when anger is moti-vated by love of your brother, by love of what is right for people, by what is called from you by love for God, is it constructive, creative anger.

How do we fulfill this in day-to-day living? Here are a few suggestions: Slow down your temper, delay your anger, set a later time for settling it after your emotions cool. Always settle it on schedule, put it off while you do a long slow burn. Keep close tab. Balance your anger ledger at the end of each day.

"Don't let the sun go down upon your wrath."

Be honest about your anger. Do talk it out. Examine your motives. Be critical of your anger emotions.

We have examined in this chapter, the causes, types, and effects of anger upon our daily relationships. The problem of handling this powerful human emotion will of lesser burden to the Christian who fully accepts uses the power of prayer and the Word of God. The following checklist may be of some help (adapted from Wright, *Christian Marriage and Family Relation-*).

Do you have a temper?
Do you control it?
Do others know when you are angry?
Describe how you feel when angry.
Does your anger surge up quickly?
Do you hold resentments?
Does your anger affect you physically?
Have you ever hit someone or something?
When was the last time?

for you to verbalize your feelings. These methods may sound strange but they should not be discounted because they have helped many people overcome their difficulties with this emotion.

The final method of dealing with anger is to **confess** it. This is perhaps the best method, especially if it is coupled with an intelligent and healthy use of suppression or self-control. Confess the fact that you are angry —to yourself, to God, and to the person involved. Don't say, "You're making me angry." The individual is not making you angry. You are responsible for your own emotional reaction toward him. You could say, "The way our discussion is going, I'm getting angry. I'm not sure that's the best reaction so perhaps we could start over in our discussion." Or, "I'm sorry but I'm angry. What can I do now so we can resolve our differences?" Try admitting and confessing your anger.

James suggests that we confess our faults to one another. This *does not mean* that all of our anger is sinful or wrong! Just the admission of being angry can help you release the feeling and get the message across in an acceptable manner to the person involved. Augsburger writes about the problem in *Caring Enough to Confront*.

Explosive anger is "the curse of interpersonal relations." Vented anger may ventilate feelings and provide instant, though temporary, release for tortured emotions, but it does little for relationships.

Clearly expressed anger is something different. Clear statements of anger feelings and angry demands can slice through emotional barriers or communications tangles and establish contact.

Anger is a part of our lives which can be controlled and directed. Consider these principles for dealing with anger.

1. Be aware of your emotional reactions. Recognize the emotion and admit to yourself that you are feeling irritated or angry. Do not repress or deny the feeling. Admitting it does not mean that you have to act on it.

2. Try to understand why you are angry. What brought it about? Can you isolate the cause or reason? Is it one that occurs often?

3. Can *you* create other situations in which anger won't occur? What were you doing that might have contributed to this problem or difficulty? Did you do anything to cause the other person to react in such a way that you became angry?

4. Ask yourself, "Is anger the best response?" You can be rational at this point and discuss this question with yourself. What are the consequences of becoming angry and letting it out? Write down your answer. Can you think of a better response? Write that down. What would be accomplished by kindness, sympathy, and understanding toward the other person? Can you confess your feelings to him?

5. Is your anger the kind that rises too soon? If so, when you start to get angry take some deep breaths or count to ten. Concentrate on the strengths and positive qualities of the other person instead of his defects. Remember that it is possible to control your thoughts. (*See* Ephesians 4:23; 1 Peter 1:13.)

6. Do you find yourself being critical of others? What does

this do for you? Be less suspicious of th
Listen to what he says and feels. Evalua
instead of condemning him. Does you
anger come from a desire to make you
Are your opinions always accurate or
proved? The other person may have
you. Slow down in your speech and
others. Watch your gestures and expr
convey rejection and criticism of the
you express appreciation and praise i

7. You may have a time when your a
legitimate. Plan ahead how you wil
in such a way that the other person
say. Use timing, tact, and have a de
person instead of tearing him dov

8. Find a friend with whom you can t
and gain some insight from his su
you feel and ask for his guidanc

9. Spend time praying for the difficu
your feelings. Openly admit yo
for His help. Understand and n
that speak of anger and those
should behave toward others.

David Augsburger offers so
help us control our anger in *E*

1. Be angry, but beware—you
than when in anger. Self-control
decreases, common sense usuall

2. Be angry, but be aware—th
it sours into resentment, hatre

10. How do you control your anger?
11. Who taught you?
12. Are others afraid of your anger?
13. Are others afraid of your criticism?
14. What causes your anger or criticism?
15. How often do you get angry?
16. What are you dissatisfied with in life?
17. How often do you get mad at people or things?
18. What do you do about your anger?
19. How do you handle anger directed toward you?
20. Do you repress your anger?
21. Do you suppress it?
22. Do you express or confess it?
23. What Scriptures can help you? Write them down.
24. Do you regularly memorize Scripture?
25. Do you openly and honestly pray about your emotions?
26. Do you really expect God to help you change your emotions?
27. Do *you* want to change?

7
Your Self-Image

He who hates himself, who does not have a proper
regard for his own capacities . . . can have no respect
for others; deep within himself he will hate his brothers when he sees in them his own marred image.

JOSHUA LIEBMAN
Peace of Mind

How do you feel about yourself? When you look at
yourself in a mirror, do you have a good feeling about
the person you see? Are you satisfied with who and
what you are? Do you like yourself?

Maxwell Maltz says in *Psychocybernetics* that self-
image is "the individual's mental and spiritual concept
or 'picture' of himself." It is what a person believes
about himself, the map he consults in order to understand himself. The attitude you have toward yourself is
extremely important.

Where do we acquire these feelings about ourselves?
How do we arrive at a self-image? Why do some people
end up with a good feeling about themselves, others
with a bad feeling?

Our feelings about ourselves have their origin in the
early years of childhood, largely through our interpersonal relationships. The attitudes and opinions com-
municated to us by others, and our identification with

other people, all tend to mold the view we have of ourselves. Each of us needs to feel significant or worthwhile in the eyes of some other person.

Early in life, a person develops a variety of concepts and attitudes about himself and his world. Some of these concepts are linked to reality, others deviate from reality, producing a distorted view of one's self. A person's self-concepts are actually clusters of attitudes about himself, some favorable, some unfavorable. These clusters consist of generalizations he has made on the basis of his interactions with his environment.

Parents, brothers, and sisters are important figures in the development of our self-image. The Scriptures indicate the importance of the father's role in the development of a child's self-image as indicated by this passage.

> Fathers, do not provoke *or* irritate *or* fret your children—do not be hard on them or harass them; lest they become discouraged *and* sullen *and* morose *and* feel inferior *and* frustrated; do not break their spirit.
>
> Colossians 3:21 AMPLIFIED

The actions of his parents penetrate the life of a vulnerable child and help him form either good or bad feelings about himself.

According to Aaron J. Beck, once a particular attitude or concept has been formed, it usually influences future judgments and becomes firmly set. For example, a child who gets the notion that he is incapable, as a result of a failure or of being *called* incompetent by somebody else, may evaluate future experiences according to this belief. Each negative judgment tends to reinforce the negative belief or self-image. Thus, the vicious cycle is set in motion: each negative judgment reinforces the negative self-image which in turn reinforces a negative interpretation of future experiences which further consolidates the negative self-concept.

It is important to remember that the image a person has of himself *is* determined mostly through his interpersonal relationships. A person's self-image or self-estimate is the result of the *interpretation he makes* of his involvements with others. What really matters to this person is not what others actually think, *but what he thinks they think of him!* It is this *subjective interpretation* that is important to his self-image.

From time to time many people experience negative thoughts and feelings about themselves. But in order for a negative self-concept to be considered sick, it must be associated with a negative value judgment. Not all people who regard themselves as physically, mentally, or socially lacking in certain areas consider these traits as bad, nor are they repelled by them. They simply accept the fact of their limitations or try to change them. Some people, however, make negative value judgments based on their deficiencies and tell themselves, "I must be bad or worthless. Only bad people have these traits. It's my fault I have them. I'll always be this way, there's no hope of changing."

The attitudes that make up our self-image continually reinforce themselves as illustrated below.

The person who has a good self-image feels worthwhile and good about himself. He likes himself and accepts both his positive qualities and his weak areas. He has confidence but he is also realistic. He knows how to handle other people's reactions toward him, both positive and negative. He expects to accomplish what he is capable of doing and feels that others will respond

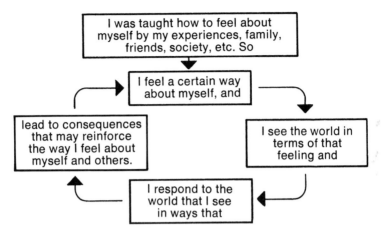

to him. He has confidence in his perceptions, ability, and judgments. He is not afraid to become involved in the lives of other people nor to open his own life to others. He is not defensive.

The person who has a poor self-image or low self-esteem is just the opposite. He lacks trust in himself and is usually apprehensive about expressing his ideas. He may withdraw and live in the shadow of others or his social group. He usually is unwilling to expose his ideas or do anything that would attract attention. He is usually overly aware of himself and has a morbid preoccupation with his problems.

His social relationships are affected. Because he has a low estimate of himself he projects this attitude onto others and thinks they must feel the same way about him. His intense feelings of inferiority limit his involvements with people. He can still be with people but he is hesitant to become honestly and openly involved with them. Since he feels other people will not want to include him in their group he is hesitant to join them for fear of rejection. He is overly sensitive to criticism for you to verbalize your feelings. These methods may sound strange but they should not be discounted because they have helped many people overcome their difficulties with this emotion.

The final method of dealing with anger is to *confess* it. This is perhaps the best method, especially if it is coupled with an intelligent and healthy use of suppression or self-control. Confess the fact that you are angry —to yourself, to God, and to the person involved. Don't say, "You're making me angry." The individual is not making you angry. You are responsible for your own emotional reaction toward him. You could say, "The way our discussion is going, I'm getting angry. I'm not sure that's the best reaction so perhaps we could start over in our discussion." Or, "I'm sorry but I'm angry. What can I do now so we can resolve our differences?" Try admitting and confessing your anger.

James suggests that we confess our faults to one another. This *does not mean* that all of our anger is sinful or wrong! Just the admission of being angry can help you release the feeling and get the message across in an acceptable manner to the person involved. Augsburger writes about the problem in *Caring Enough to Confront*.

Explosive anger is "the curse of interpersonal relations." Vented anger may ventilate feelings and provide instant, though temporary, release for tortured emotions, but it does little for relationships.

Clearly expressed anger is something different. Clear statements of anger feelings and angry demands can slice through emotional barriers or communications tangles and establish contact.

Anger is a part of our lives which can be controlled and directed. Consider these principles for dealing with anger.

1. Be aware of your emotional reactions. Recognize the emotion and admit to yourself that you are feeling irritated or angry. Do not repress or deny the feeling. Admitting it does not mean that you have to act on it.

2. Try to understand why you are angry. What brought it about? Can you isolate the cause or reason? Is it one that occurs often?

3. Can *you* create other situations in which anger won't occur? What were you doing that might have contributed to this problem or difficulty? Did you do anything to cause the other person to react in such a way that you became angry?

4. Ask yourself, "Is anger the best response?" You can be rational at this point and discuss this question with yourself. What are the consequences of becoming angry and letting it out? Write down your answer. Can you think of a better response? Write that down. What would be accomplished by kindness, sympathy, and understanding toward the other person? Can you confess your feelings to him?

5. Is your anger the kind that rises too soon? If so, when you start to get angry take some deep breaths or count to ten. Concentrate on the strengths and positive qualities of the other person instead of his defects. Remember that it is possible to control your thoughts. (*See* Ephesians 4:23; 1 Peter 1:13.)

6. Do you find yourself being critical of others? What does

this do for you? Be less suspicious of the other person. *Listen* to what he says and feels. Evaluate his comments instead of condemning him. Does your faultfinding or anger come from a desire to make yourself feel better? Are your opinions always accurate or could they be improved? The other person may have something to offer you. Slow down in your speech and reactions toward others. Watch your gestures and expressions which may convey rejection and criticism of the other person. Can you express appreciation and praise in place of criticism?

7. You may have a time when your anger or criticism is legitimate. Plan ahead how you will express it and do it in such a way that the other person can accept what you say. Use timing, tact, and have a desire to help the other person instead of tearing him down.

8. Find a friend with whom you can talk over your feelings and gain some insight from his suggestions. Admit how you feel and ask for his guidance.

9. Spend time praying for the difficulty that you have with your feelings. Openly admit your situation to God. Ask for His help. Understand and memorize the Scriptures that speak of anger and those that speak of how we should behave toward others. Put them into practice.

David Augsburger offers some additional ways to help us control our anger in *Be All You Can Be.*

1. Be angry, but beware—you are never more vulnerable than when in anger. Self-control is at an all-time low, reason decreases, common sense usually forsakes you.

2. Be angry, but be aware—that anger quickly turns bitter, it sours into resentment, hatred, malice, evil temper, and

even violence unless it is controlled by love.

3. Be angry, but only to be kind. Only when anger is motivated by love of your brother, by love of what is right for people, by what is called from you by love for God, is it constructive, creative anger.

How do we fulfill this in day-to-day living? Here are a few suggestions: Slow down your temper, delay your anger, set a later time for settling it after your emotions cool. Always settle it on schedule, put it off while you do a long slow burn. Keep close tab. Balance your anger ledger at the end of each day.

"Don't let the sun go down upon your wrath."

Be honest about your anger. Do talk it out. Examine your motives. Be critical of your anger emotions.

We have examined in this chapter, the causes, types, and effects of anger upon our daily relationships. The problem of handling this powerful human emotion will be of lesser burden to the Christian who fully accepts and uses the power of prayer and the Word of God. The following checklist may be of some help (adapted from Wright, *Christian Marriage and Family Relationship*).

1. Do you have a temper?
2. Do you control it?
3. Do others know when you are angry?
4. Describe how you feel when angry.
5. Does your anger surge up quickly?
6. Do you hold resentments?
7. Does your anger affect you physically?
8. Have you ever hit someone or something?
9. When was the last time?

10. How do you control your anger?
11. Who taught you?
12. Are others afraid of your anger?
13. Are others afraid of your criticism?
14. What causes your anger or criticism?
15. How often do you get angry?
16. What are you dissatisfied with in life?
17. How often do you get mad at people or things?
18. What do you do about your anger?
19. How do you handle anger directed toward you?
20. Do you repress your anger?
21. Do you suppress it?
22. Do you express or confess it?
23. What Scriptures can help you? Write them down.
24. Do you regularly memorize Scripture?
25. Do you openly and honestly pray about your emotions?
26. Do you really expect God to help you change your emotions?
27. Do *you* want to change?

7
Your Self-Image

He who hates himself, who does not have a proper
regard for his own capacities . . . can have no respect
for others; deep within himself he will hate his brothers when he sees in them his own marred image.

JOSHUA LIEBMAN
Peace of Mind

How do you feel about yourself? When you look at
yourself in a mirror, do you have a good feeling about
the person you see? Are you satisfied with who and
what you are? Do you like yourself?

Maxwell Maltz says in *Psychocybernetics* that self-
image is "the individual's mental and spiritual concept
or 'picture' of himself." It is what a person believes
about himself, the map he consults in order to understand himself. The attitude you have toward yourself is
extremely important.

Where do we acquire these feelings about ourselves?
How do we arrive at a self-image? Why do some people
end up with a good feeling about themselves, others
with a bad feeling?

Our feelings about ourselves have their origin in the
early years of childhood, largely through our interpersonal relationships. The attitudes and opinions com-
municated to us by others, and our identification with

other people, all tend to mold the view we have of ourselves. Each of us needs to feel significant or worthwhile in the eyes of some other person.

Early in life, a person develops a variety of concepts and attitudes about himself and his world. Some of these concepts are linked to reality, others deviate from reality, producing a distorted view of one's self. A person's self-concepts are actually clusters of attitudes about himself, some favorable, some unfavorable. These clusters consist of generalizations he has made on the basis of his interactions with his environment.

Parents, brothers, and sisters are important figures in the development of our self-image. The Scriptures indicate the importance of the father's role in the development of a child's self-image as indicated by this passage.

> Fathers, do not provoke *or* irritate *or* fret your children—do not be hard on them or harass them; lest they become discouraged *and* sullen *and* morose *and* feel inferior *and* frustrated; do not break their spirit.
> Colossians 3:21 AMPLIFIED

The actions of his parents penetrate the life of a vulnerable child and help him form either good or bad feelings about himself.

According to Aaron J. Beck, once a particular attitude or concept has been formed, it usually influences future judgments and becomes firmly set. For example, a child who gets the notion that he is incapable, as a result of a failure or of being *called* incompetent by somebody else, may evaluate future experiences according to this belief. Each negative judgment tends to reinforce the negative belief or self-image. Thus, the vicious cycle is set in motion: each negative judgment reinforces the negative self-image which in turn reinforces a negative interpretation of future experiences which further consolidates the negative self-concept.

It is important to remember that the image a person has of himself *is* determined mostly through his interpersonal relationships. A person's self-image or self-estimate is the result of the *interpretation he makes* of his involvements with others. What really matters to this person is not what others actually think, *but what he thinks they think of him!* It is this *subjective interpretation* that is important to his self-image.

From time to time many people experience negative thoughts and feelings about themselves. But in order for a negative self-concept to be considered sick, it must be associated with a negative value judgment. Not all people who regard themselves as physically, mentally, or socially lacking in certain areas consider these traits as bad, nor are they repelled by them. They simply accept the fact of their limitations or try to change them. Some people, however, make negative value judgments based on their deficiencies and tell themselves, "I must be bad or worthless. Only bad people have these traits. It's my fault I have them. I'll always be this way, there's no hope of changing."

The attitudes that make up our self-image continually reinforce themselves as illustrated below.

The person who has a good self-image feels worthwhile and good about himself. He likes himself and accepts both his positive qualities and his weak areas. He has confidence but he is also realistic. He knows how to handle other people's reactions toward him, both positive and negative. He expects to accomplish what he is capable of doing and feels that others will respond

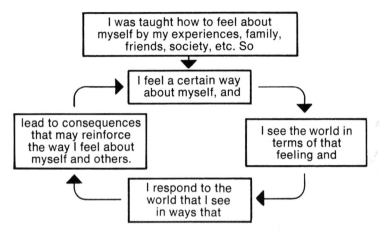

to him. He has confidence in his perceptions, ability, and judgments. He is not afraid to become involved in the lives of other people nor to open his own life to others. He is not defensive.

The person who has a poor self-image or low self-esteem is just the opposite. He lacks trust in himself and is usually apprehensive about expressing his ideas. He may withdraw and live in the shadow of others or his social group. He usually is unwilling to expose his ideas or do anything that would attract attention. He is usually overly aware of himself and has a morbid preoccupation with his problems.

His social relationships are affected. Because he has a low estimate of himself he projects this attitude onto others and thinks they must feel the same way about him. His intense feelings of inferiority limit his involvements with people. He can still be with people but he is hesitant to become honestly and openly involved with them. Since he feels other people will not want to include him in their group he is hesitant to join them for fear of rejection. He is overly sensitive to criticism and reads things into conversations and situations that are not there. Often he displays a facade with others and they never really know him or realize that he feels so bad about himself.

Unfortunately, today it is fashionable to play the game of creating false impressions. Sidney Jourard calls this the "poker game of society" in which we bluff one another with our multitude of masks. This in turn creates a psychological curtain between people. We enclose ourselves in protective armor and we learn to play the game of deception well. The fear of letting oneself be known to others and perhaps experiencing their rejection, criticism, or even acceptance, impinges upon man's honesty to himself, to others, and to God.

Adam started us down this road of deception and because of that we all have the potential to experience this false life in some manner. We thus see portrayed this inception of dishonesty:

> Then the eyes of both were opened, and they knew that they were naked; and they sewed fig leaves together and made themselves aprons. And they heard the sound of the Lord God walking in the garden in the cool of the day, and the man and his wife hid themselves from the presence of the Lord God among the trees of the garden. But the Lord God called to the man, and said to him, "Where are you?" And he said, "I heard the sound of thee in the garden, and I was afraid, because I was naked; and I hid myself."
>
> Genesis 3:7–10 RSV

God did not create us to be this way—man made the choice. *This alone I have found, that God, when He made man, made him straightforward, but man in-*

vents endless subtleties of his own (Ecclesiastes 7:29 NEB).

As one man put it, "I am afraid to tell you who I am because if I tell you who I am, you might not like who I am and that's all I've got!" John Powell elaborates in *Why Am I Afraid to Tell You Who I Am?*

None of us want to be a fraud or to live a lie; none of us want to be a sham, a phony, but the fears that we experience and the risks that honest self-communication would involve seem so intense to us that seeking refuge in our roles, masks and games becomes an almost natural reflex action.

Inner scars, pains and fears of the past block our sharing ourselves with others. From infancy on, a person learns to erect a pleasing or false veneer in order to protect and in many cases to advance himself in his society. "We conceal our person behind a protective barrier," says Paul Tournier in *The Meaning of Persons.* "We let it be seen only through the bars. We display certain of its aspects, others we carefully hide."

Pretense and the pattern of deception have been so refined and perfected by some people that not only have they deceived others, but they have tended to lose touch with their real selves! How unfortunate this is! And it leads us into the insidious pastime of trying (through falsehood) to get others to like us. But it doesn't work! As we see in *Normal Neurosis: The Adjusted American* by Snell and Gail Putney:

The person who is caught up in the quest for indirect self-acceptance is more concerned with making a favorable impression on others than with seeing an honest reflection of himself. He attempts to manipulate the way he appears to others. Consequently he cannot credit any favorable image they may reflect, for he has good reason to think that what he sees is only his most flattering angle.

Moreover, he is likely to become preoccupied with the limitations he is struggling to conceal from others, with the result that these "defects" loom disproportionately large in his self-image. The person who seeks indirect self-acceptance thus begins by trying to manipulate the image he presents to others and ends by having a distorted self-image, in which his defects are magnified.

All of us are dependent upon our relationships with other individuals. No one exists as a completely separate personality, alone and cut off from others. Our personalities are formed in relation to those about us, a process which continues throughout life. Isolating oneself from others brings stagnation and ultimately regression and retreat. It just reinforces a poor self-image.

People with a low self-image fear that they are failures. In order to prove they are not they often shy away from competitive ventures. Cynicism often sets in, as is pointed out by Arthur DeJong in *Making It to Adulthood.*

To prove his worth to others and to himself, the person with low self-esteem often takes on the image of "worker" or "helper" or both. The worker goes at his work feverishly and with an eye to perfection. The helper feels worthwhile when he has helped someone and when that person responds affirmatively. Since he is never convinced of his worth, the person repeats this pattern endlessly. Indeed, it becomes a need, and therefore a personality trait.

Because the person with low self-esteem wishes to be ac-

cepted by others, both to prove his worth and to gain interpersonal relationships, he is often guided more by what he
thinks will please others than by his own desires, or by what
he thinks is right. He is not his own man, but rather a victim
of his feelings and needs. Down deep he hates himself because of this lack of integrity. Thus he is caught in a vicious
circle.

How do you feel about yourself? What guidelines can
we use to develop a positive self-image? Must we look
at ourselves through our own eyes with our biases and
distortions, or is there another way? The Apostle Paul
writes:

> For by the grace (unmerited favor of God) given to
> me I warn every one among you not to estimate *and*
> think of himself more highly than he ought—not to
> have an exaggerated opinion of his own importance;
> but to rate his ability with sober judgment, each ac-
> cording to the degree of faith apportioned by God to
> him.
>
> Romans 12:3 AMPLIFIED

Paul suggests that we use certain guidelines to evaluate ourselves. He says we are not to think too highly of
ourselves. By implication it would be just as bad to
think too lowly of ourselves for that is a negative form
of pride. He suggests that we think realistically.

Paul had a very realistic view of himself. He often saw
himself as a great sinner. But he never described himself as a great sinner without at the same time referring
to the grace of God which forgave his sins, accepted
him, and enabled him to be useful for God's service.
Paul never simply sat down and brooded about his sins.

Whenever he thought about his sins, he thought about the grace of God! In 1 Timothy 1:15 KJV, for example, Paul calls himself the chief of sinners, but in the same context he describes salvation: . . . *faithful [is the] saying, and worthy of all acceptation, that Christ Jesus came into the world to save sinners; of whom I am chief.* In Ephesians 3:8 KJV he contrasts his feeling of unworthiness with the privileged position to which God has called him: *Unto me, who am less than the least of all saints, is this grace given, that I should preach among the Gentiles the unsearchable riches of Christ.* Paul also expresses his deep feelings about the fact that he was once a persecutor. Yet he maintains a positive self-image because of what the grace of God has done for him and is still doing through him.

> For I am the least of the apostles, that am not meet [fit] to be called an apostle, because I persecuted the church of God. But by the grace of God I am what I am: and his grace which was bestowed upon me was not found vain: but I laboured more abundantly than they all; yet not I, but the grace of God which was with me.
>
> 1 Corinthians 15:9, 10 KJV

Though Paul can look back to aspects of his former life of which he is now ashamed, he does not continue to brood or dwell on these things; he has learned to *forget the things which are behind (see* Philippians 3:13). Despite his deep sense of sin, Paul had a positive self-image. He saw himself as someone upon whom God had given His grace, whom God had enabled and was still enabling to live a fruitful life for Christ, and whom God so continued to fill with His Spirit that his life could be an example to others.

Paul was aware of the trap of evaluating ourselves in terms of the estimation of others. He suggests that we spend less time evaluating ourselves and other people and leave this to God!

> But (as for me personally) it matters very little to me that I should be put on trial by you, . . . *and* that you or any other human tribunal should investigate *and* question *and* cross-question me. I do not even put myself on trial *and* judge myself. I am not conscious of anything against myself, *and* I feel blameless; but I am not vindicated *and* acquitted before God on that account. It is the Lord [Himself] Who examines *and* judges me. So do not make any hasty *or* premature judgments before the time when the Lord comes [again], for He will both bring to light the secret things that are (now hidden) in darkness, and disclose *and* expose the (secret) aims (motives and purposes) of hearts. Then every man will receive his (due) commendation from God.
>
> 1 Corinthians 4:3–5 AMPLIFIED

Did you notice the word used here in the last verse? It was not that you and I will receive our condemnation! It is *commendation*. Often we pour energy into condemning ourselves but God is going to commend us! The person with a poor self-image searches out Scriptures to reinforce his own feelings of condemnation. But the Word of God portrays the greatest amount of acceptance we could ever imagine.

> Therefore, since we are justified—acquitted, declared righteous, and given a right standing with God—

through faith, let us [grasp the fact that we] have [the peace of reconciliation] to hold *and* to enjoy, peace with God through our Lord Jesus Christ, the Messiah, the Anointed One.

Romans 5:1 AMPLIFIED

Therefore [there is] now no condemnation—no adjudging guilty of wrong—for those who are in Christ Jesus. . . .

Romans 8:1 AMPLIFIED

Romans 8:16,17 tells us that we who know Jesus Christ are joint heirs with Him. We have full sonship with Him. We have been and we are *accepted* and *acceptable!*

Tom Skinner makes this point so well in his book *Black and Free:* "Christ has given me true dignity. . . . You see, I am a son of God. . . . As a son of God, I have all the rights and privileges that go with that rank. I have the dignity that goes with being a member of the royal family of God."

Because God loves and accepts us through Jesus Christ, it is possible and necessary for us to love and accept ourselves. But the question is often raised, "Isn't it wrong to love oneself? Isn't that unscriptural?" The answer is an emphatic *no!* God tells us that we are to love ourselves! He created us. The image of God is within us! If we hate ourselves in some way then are we not hating God Himself?

"But was not the image of God taken away because of the Fall of man?" someone will ask. The answer again is no. Even after man sinned, the image of God remained in him. It was marred with sin, but there was still something about man which was good and like

God. The image of God in fallen man is effaced but not completely erased.

Many verses declare men to be good by nature insofar as they are the creation of God. Paul told Timothy, *For everything created by God is good . . .* (1 Timothy 4:4 RSV). To Titus, Paul said, *To the pure all things are pure . . .* (Titus 1:15 RSV). Not only is there some good in us, but even evil men can *do* good things. Jesus said, *If you then, who are evil, know how to give good gifts to your children, how much more will your Father who is in heaven . . .* (Matthew 7:11 RSV).

Regarding his sinful self, Paul said, *. . . I can will what is right, but* (he added in complaint) *I cannot do it. . . . For I delight in the law of God, in my inmost self* (Romans 7:18,22 RSV). Despite his sinful tendencies and inability to do all the good things he wanted to do, Paul recognized within his sinful self something which could at least will what is right.

Does this mean we are to like everything we think or do or say? Not at all. We can dislike our actions and defects and still accept ourselves as being of worth. In place of castigating ourselves and wallowing in excessive guilt, we must confess our wrongs, ask for forgiveness and go on.

Some people argue that the Scriptures indicate we are to be hard on ourselves even to the point of having a negative self-image. They cling to passages such as the following to support their view.

> . . . . Instead, in the true spirit of humility (lowliness of mind) let each regard the others as better than *and* superior to himself—thinking more highly of one another than you do of yourselves. Let each of you esteem *and* look upon *and* be concerned for not

[merely] his own interests, but also each for the interests of others.

Philippians 2:3,4 AMPLIFIED

The question has been raised whether this biblical passage implies a type of negative self-image. Does this mean, in order to be good Christians, we must think of ourselves as inferior to others?

Perhaps here is a question of interpretation. Philippians 2:3 ASV says, *doing nothing through faction or through vainglory, but in lowliness of mind each counting other better than himself. . . .* The Phillips Modern English paraphrase captures the spirit of this verse: *Never act from motives of rivalry or personal vanity, but in humility think more of one another than you do of yourselves.* The emphasis is not that I must demean myself or think of myself as inferior to someone else. Instead I must not seek my own honor at someone else's expense, I must be more concerned to honor or praise others than I am to have others praise me, or as in Romans 12:10 KJV, . . . *in honour preferring one another.* I must be more eager to see someone else be honored than I am to see myself so recognized. This *does not* imply, however, that I need to despise or deprecate myself. To the contrary, it requires a pretty healthy kind of self-confidence or self-esteem for a person to be more concerned for the other man's honor than for his own.

A similar thought is found in Colossians 3:12 AMPLIFIED:

Clothe yourselves therefore, as . . . His own chosen ones, . . . purified *and* holy and well-beloved [. . . by putting on behavior marked by] tenderhearted pity

and mercy, kind feeling, a lowly opinion of yourselves. . . .

Lowly does not mean to have a poor self-image or to
dislike yourself. It refers to the spirit in which we accept God's dealing with us as good, and, therefore without disputing or resistance. We don't fight against God.

We are to hate the selfish tendencies and actions in
ourselves, but we are to love ourselves. This legitimate
self-love is clearly implied in Scripture's command to
Love your neighbor as yourself.

Why should men love themselves? There are several
reasons. First, because men are like God. As we have
already discussed, the Word of God teaches that man is
made in the image and likeness of God. To hate oneself
is actually to hate God.

Second, men ought to love themselves because it is
the basis of their love for others. The love of another
person is based on one's love of self. If one does not
properly love himself, he cannot properly love others.
There really is no other way.

Conversely, failure to love others in the right way is
based on a failure to love oneself in a proper way. Since
the Bible commands Christians to love others and since
love of self is the basis for loving others, then it is clear
that one needs to learn to love himself correctly. The
Christian should not love himself in an egotistical way,
but for the sake of loving others. One of the reasons for
cultivating self-love is that it will help us love others
better.

Third, since the Bible teaches that to love others is to
love God, it is important to learn a proper self-love so
that one can love others more and thereby love God
better. Jesus said, . . . *as you did it* [*showed love*] *to one*

of the least of these my brethren, you did it to me
(Matthew 25:40 RSV). John wrote, *If any one says, "I
love God," and hates his brother, he is a liar* . . . (1 John
4:20 RSV). A healthy self-love as a basis for loving other
men can be one way of increasing one's love for God.

Finally, a Christian should love himself because God
loves him. God loves man and wishes to reconcile him
to Himself. Sinful men are redeemable and valuable to
God. God loves all men and sent His Son to be the
sacrifice for their sins. If God so loves sinful men for the
redeemable value in them, then we ought to love these
men too, including ourselves.

Dr. Lloyd Ahlem in *Do I Have to Be Me?* so clearly
summarizes what God has done for us.

The writers of the Scriptures are careful to point out that
when God looks at you in Jesus Christ, He sees you as a
brother to His own Son. Because of the work of Christ, all the
ugliness of humanity is set aside. God has absolutely no attitude of condemnation toward man. You are worth all of
God's attention. If you were the only person in the whole
world, it would be worth God's effort to make Himself known
to you and to love you. He gives you freely the status and
adequacy of an heir to the universe.

This is agape love, the unmerited, unconditional favor of
God for man. We achieve our adequacy through this unceas-
ing love. We do not *become* sufficient, approved, or adequate; rather we are *declared to be* such! When we believe
this, we become achievers and humanitarians as an effect, a
by-product of our new-found selves.

This gift has been extended to each and every person. Your part is to respond by accepting. This also
means that you begin to live a life of faith. You base

your self-concept on the fact of what God has done and accept it by faith. This means challenging some of your built-in attitudes and feelings. Man cannot live by feelings, but by faith.

Unfortunately, many people cannot accept this free gift from God, and they cannot accept a gift of love from other people either, as Ahlem adds:

We insist on bartering when He (God) would give us His gifts freely. He offers us forgiveness, status, adequacy, direction in life. Instead of responding with thanks and love, we insist on earning the gift or trading something for it. We become so religious nobody can stand us. Or we refuse His gift and say that we do not deserve it. Or we become so aseptically moral that no needy human can touch us. We forget so quickly that Jesus was the one who took care of any shortage of payment we owe, or any bartering that had to be done, He gave Himself so that we could freely receive. You can be adequate. You can be guilt-free! Accept His love, your doubts about the truth of the matter will vanish when you do. He will put His spirit within you, and honest joy will surprise you.

When a person has accepted adequacy as a gift, he immediately perceives a new standard for achievement. No longer does the criterion of human performance apply, but rather the measure of faithfulness judges us. This is the fair standard, the one that stimulates everyone, frustrates no one, and is administered by the providential will of God.

The teaching of the Word of God gives sufficient basis for a person to have a positive feeling about himself. But the difficulty arises in trying to effect a change from a negative to a positive concept. The teaching *As a man thinks in his heart, so is he,* is so reflected in our self-image (*see* Proverbs 23:7).

Perhaps you are one who has suffered from feelings of inadequacy. Now you are seeking to fully receive God's love and acceptance so you can believe that you are worthwhile. There are several practical steps you can take to begin building a healthy concept.

Read the Scriptures which were mentioned earlier: Romans 5:1; 8:1,16,17. Read, reread, and study them until you know them completely and *believe* they are speaking about you. Accept them by faith without being concerned about your feelings. You might have a tendency to say, "Well, I don't *feel* justified" or "I don't *feel* that I'm not condemned." You cannot rely on your own feelings. Instead, ask yourself, "If I really did believe these verses, how would I be feeling and how would I be acting?" After you have answered this question, begin to act as you have decided you would if these verses were a part of your life. If you change your actions, many of your feelings will also change.

Begin to practice a life-style of openness and honesty with yourself and other people. The starting point for a life of honesty and disclosure begins, not in our relationships with man, but in our relationship with God. We begin to acknowledge to God our personal struggles, doubts, and betrayals. We share with Him that we are weak in our witness, that we are proud of our accomplishments and have difficulty giving Him the credit for our successes. Confession of sin is an essential condition for health—spiritual as well as psychological. But it can become a morbid and unhealthy pastime if there is too much concentration upon sins, especially sins that are past and have been confessed, forgiven, and forgotten. Paul admonished his readers, . . . *forgetting what lies behind and straining forward to what*

lies ahead, I press on . . . (Philippians 3:13,14 RSV).
The Scriptures vividly depict the inner anguish of those who try to cover or hide their sins.

> When I declared not my sin, my body wasted away through my groaning all day long. For day and night thy hand was heavy upon me; my strength was dried up as by the heat of summer. *Selah.*
>
> I acknowledged my sin to thee, and I did not hide my iniquity; I said, "I will confess my transgressions to the Lord"; then thou didst forgive the guilt of my sin. *Selah.*
>
> Psalms 32:3–5 RSV

Sin really cannot be hidden. There are no secrets we can keep from God. Jesus spoke of this when He said:

> Nothing is covered up that will not be revealed, or hidden that will not be known. Whatever you have said in the dark shall be heard in the light, and what you have whispered in private rooms shall be proclaimed upon the housetops.
>
> Luke 12:2,3 RSV

The purpose of confession of sin is perhaps twofold as expressed in Proverbs 28:13 RSV, *He who conceals his transgressions will not prosper, but he who confesses and forsakes them will obtain mercy.* Forgiveness and forsaking are inseparable. When confession is honestly made before God there are results.

Psalms graphically illustrate that a *covering* of sin will occur, if confession precedes it. The covering or blotting out of the sin is accomplished wholly and completely by God.

Blessed is he whose transgression is forgiven, whose sin is covered. I acknowledged my sin to thee, and I did not hide my iniquity; I said, "I will confess my transgressions to the Lord"; then thou didst forgive the guilt of my sin.

Psalms 32:1,5 RSV

The Scriptures say that God *blots them out, casts them behind His back, buries them and remembers them no more.* If man covers sins they haunt him. But if He recalls and brings them out into the open with shame and remorse, *God* forgives and covers them.

When man first opens himself to God he sees himself, begins to know himself, and through Jesus Christ discovers the healing and filling of his defects. By experiencing the unconditional acceptance of God, man gains the courage to open himself to others and begins to overcome the fear of rejection.

And thus the adventure begins! Our masks are slowly removed in God's presence and we find that He accepts and loves us. In turn He helps us shed these masks in our relationships with others. In this process we begin to discover ourselves and attempt to understand the complexities of our lives. Only through the extended hands of Christ is this fully possible. Scripture urges us to look within and discover what we are like.

Behold, Thou dost desire truth in the innermost being. And in the hidden part Thou wilt make me know wisdom.

Psalms 51:6 NAS

Test yourselves *to see* if you are in the faith; examine yourselves! Or do you not recognize this about your-

selves, that Jesus Christ is in you—unless indeed you
fail the test?

2 Corinthians 13:5 NAS

God is the searcher of the innermost parts of man and
even though we search ourselves we must look to God
in faith.

. . . . For the Lord searches all hearts *and* minds and
understands all the wanderings of the thoughts. . . .

1 Chronicles 28:9 AMPLIFIED

O Lord, You have searched me (thoroughly) and have
known me. You know my downsitting and my upris-
ing; You understand my thought afar off.

Psalms 139:1, 2 AMPLIFIED

I, the Lord, search the mind, I try the heart, even to
give every man according to his ways, according to the
fruit of his doings.

Jeremiah 17:10 AMPLIFIED

For what person perceives (knows and understands)
what passes through a man's own spirit within him?
Just so no one discerns (comes to know and com-
prehend) the thoughts of God except the Spirit of
God.

1 Corinthians 2:11 AMPLIFIED

It is the action of God assisting man to uncover himself in His presence which in turn enables man to reveal
himself to another.

Reevaluate your set of values. Many people empha-
size the point that in order to be or feel worthwhile we

must achieve and overachieve. It is disastrous to measure our worth and value by what we accomplish. This usually leads to the belief that we must do better each time and do better than others. This in turn leads to competition which can destroy relationships. We do not achieve our worth by accomplishment, but just the reverse. We are able to accomplish because we are worthwhile.

Accept the fact that you are worthwhile even at the times when you are not doing your best. Some people believe they must be competent and adequate in all areas before they can consider themselves worthwhile. This is not true nor is it fair to think of yourself in this manner. Remember the concept presented by Dr. Ahlem. You do not *become* adequate. God declares you to be adequate because of what He has done for you in Jesus Christ. You're already there!

Albert Ellis, a noted psychotherapist who stresses realistic and rational thinking, has suggested in *Reason and Emotion in Psychotherapy* the following principles for the person who is caught up in trying to achieve as the basis for his adequacy.

1. A person should try to *do,* rather than kill himself trying to *do well.* He should focus on enjoying the process rather than only the result of what he does.

2. When he tries to do well, he should try to do so for his own sake rather than to please or to best others. He should be artistically and esthetically, rather than merely egotistically, involved in the results of his labors.

3. When, for his own satisfaction, he tries to do well, he should not insist on his always doing perfectly well. He

should, on most occasions, strive for *his* best rather than *the* best.

4. He should from time to time question his strivings and honestly ask himself whether he is striving for achievement in itself or for achievement for his own satisfaction.

5. If he wants to do well at any task or problem, he should learn to welcome his mistakes and errors, rather than become horrified at them, and to put them to good account. He should accept the necessity of his practicing, practicing, practicing the things he wants to succeed at; should often force himself to do what he is afraid to fail at doing; and should fully accept the fact that human beings, in general, are limited and that he, in particular, has necessary and distinct limitations.

Begin drawing some new conclusions about yourself at this particular point in your life, whether you are eighteen or fifty-eight. It may not be easy but it is definitely possible. A person with low self-esteem has already drawn certain conclusions, which are, however, for the most part faulty. Many of these conclusions have been with us for a long period of time, some since childhood. Unfortunately, therefore, some of our conclusions are childhood thoughts. Many of our conclusions are based upon our impressions of what other people thought of us and not necessarily what they *actually* thought. Our conclusions have affected our perceptions so that we tend to see only the evidence which supports our thoughts about ourselves. We see what we want to see. And then we begin to live as though those perceptions and conclusions were true.

Test these assumptions about yourself with which you have been living. If you are shy and feel that people will not accept you into their group, have you ever tested that conclusion? Many people don't even try and those who do, probably by their hesitancy and insecure manner, give such a poor impression that people do not respond to them. Arthur DeJong illustrates this process as follows (*italics* added):

A person may look into the snack bar and see a group of students chatting over coffee. He would like to join them. Instead of actually joining them, he shifts to his imagination. He toys *in his imagination* with joining them. *In his imagination,* he finds that they do not wish to have him around. *In his imagination,* it turns out to be an abortive attempt, not worth the rejection that he receives. Because it turns out this way *in his imagination,* he does not try it out *in reality.* And yet he uses this evidence *from his imagination* to support the hypothesis. It appears to him that the evidence confirms his feelings, when actually, much, if not all, of that evidence is in his imagination.

Testing assumptions and false conclusions involves risk. But how can you improve unless you are willing to run the risk? I once read a sign that read REMEMBER THE TURTLE: HE MAKES PROGRESS ONLY WHEN HIS NECK IS OUT! Take the misdirected energy that is used in imagining the worst and use it to plan exactly what you are going to say and do as you enter a group. The chances for a positive reaction are very high. David Johnson explains in *Reaching Out:*

There is much evidence that healthy relationships are based upon self-disclosure. If you hide how you are reacting to the other person, your concealment can sicken the relationship. The energy you pour into hiding adds to the stress of the relationship and dulls your awareness of your own inner experience, thus decreasing your ability to disclose your reactions even when it is perfectly safe and appropriate to do so. Hiding your reactions from others through fear of rejection and conflict or through feelings of shame and guilt leads to loneliness. Being silent is not being strong; strength is the willingness to take risks in the relationship, to disclose yourself with the intention of building a better relationship.

When man is open to God, to others and to himself he grows and moves ahead in his life. He is willing to progress and does so for he no longer seeks to hide. No longer does he say, "And I hid myself. I was afraid."

Begin right now to focus your strengths and positive qualities. Take a piece of paper and list each one of them. If you cannot think of very many, ask some close friends to help you. Do not mention any negative traits, assumed or real. This is a time to look at the positive qualities that make up your life. Why has God allowed you to have the strengths that you have? In what way can you use these strengths for his service? How can you use these strengths to rebuild some of the weak areas of your life?

Bibliography

Ahlem, Lloyd H. *Do I Have to Be Me?* Glendale, California: Regal Books (G/L Publications), 1973.

Augsburger, David. *Be All You Can Be*. Carol Stream, Illinois: Creation House, 1970.

Augsburger, David. *Caring Enough to Confront*. Glendale, California: Regal Books, 1973.

Augsburger, David. *Seventy Times Seven*. Chicago: Moody Press, 1970.

Beck, Aaron T. M.D. *Depression: Causes and Treatment*. Philadelphia: University of Pennsylvania Press, 1967.

Cammer, Leonard. *Up From Depression*. New York: Simon & Schuster, 1969.

Collins, Vincent P. *Me, Myself and You*. St. Meinrad, Indiana: Abbey Press, 1969.

DeJong, Arthur J. *Making It to Adulthood*. Philadelphia: Westminister Press, 1972.

Eavey, C.B. *Principles of Mental Health for Christian Living*. Chicago: Moody Press, 1957.

Ellis, Albert. *Reason and Emotion in Psychotherapy*. Secaucus, New Jersey: Lyle Stuart, 1962.

Fischer, Loren. *Highway to Dynamic Living*. Scottsdale, Arizona: People on the Go, 1969.

Garrison, Webb. "The Joy of Memorizing Scripture." *Christianity Today*, November 25, 1966, p. 13.

Gockel, Herman. *Answer to Anxiety*. St. Louis, Missouri:

Concordia Publishing House, 1965.

Hadfield, James A. *Psychology and Morals.* New York: Methuen, Harper & Row, 1964.

Haggai, John E. *How to Win Over Worry.* Grand Rapids, Michigan: Zondervan Publishing House, 1967.

Hope, Norman V. "How to Be Good and Mad." *Christianity Today,* July 19, 1968, p. 3.

Hurnard, Hannah. *Winged Life.* Portland, Oregon: Artype Services, 1972.

Hyder, O. Quentin M.D. *The Christian's Handbook of Psychiatry.* Old Tappan, New Jersey: Fleming H. Revell Co., 1971.

Johnson, David W. *Reaching Out: Interpersonal Effectiveness and Self-Actualization.* Englewood Cliffs, New Jersey: Prentice Hall, 1972.

Kraines, Samuel H. and Thetford, Eloise S. *Help for the Depressed.* Springfield, Illinois: Charles C Thomas, 1972.

Lee, Earl G. *The Cycle of Victorious Living.* Kansas City, Missouri: Beacon Hill Press, 1971.

Lehner, George F. and Kube, Ella. *The Dynamics of Personal Adjustment.* Englewood Cliffs, New Jersey: Prentice Hall, 1964.

Lewis, C. S. *Mere Christianity.* Riverside, New Jersey: Macmillan Publishing Co., 1952.

Liebman, Joshua Loth. *Peace of Mind.* New York: Simon & Schuster, 1965.

Lloyd-Jones, Martyn. *From Fear to Faith.* London: Inter-Varsity Fellowship, 1953.

Lloyd-Jones, Martyn. *Spiritual Depression.* Grand Rapids, Michigan: William B. Eerdmans Publishing Co., 1965.

Lloyd-Jones, D. Martyn. *Studies in the Sermon on the Mount.* Grand Rapids, Michigan: William B. Eerdmans Publishing Co., 1960.

McMillen, S.I. *None of These Diseases.* Old Tappan, New

Jersey: Fleming H. Revell Co., 1972.

Madow, Leo. *Anger: How to Recognize and Cope With It.* New York: Charles Scribner's Sons, 1972.

Maltz, Maxwell. *Psychocybernetics.* New York: Essandess, Simon & Schuster, 1960.

Menninger, William. "Behind Many Flaws of Society. . . ." *National Observer,* August 31, 1964, p. 18.

Moore, Wilber E. *Creative and Critical Thinking.* Boston: Houghton Mifflin Co., 1967.

Osborne, Cecil. *The Art of Understanding Yourself.* Grand Rapids, Michigan: Zondervan Publishing House, 1968.

Powell, John. *Why Am I Afraid to Love?* Chicago: Argus Communications, 1967.

Powell, John. *Why Am I Afraid to Tell You Who I Am?* Chicago: Argus Communications, 1969.

Putney, Snell and Gail J. *Normal Neurosis: The Adjusted American.* New York: Harper & Row Publishers, 1964.

Sullivan, Harry S. *The Psychiatric Interview.* New York: W. W. Norton & Co., 1954.

Tournier, Paul. *The Meaning of Persons.* New York: Harper & Row Publishers, 1957.

Tozer, A. W. *Born After Midnight.* Harrisburg, Pennsylvania: Christian Publications.

Vold, James. "God's Cure for Emotional Depression." *Moody Monthly Magazine,* March 1968.

Wallace, J. MacDonald. *Relaxation, a Key to Better Living.* New York: International Publications Service, 1965.

Wright, Norman. *Christian Marriage and Family Relationship.* Glendale, California: Church Press, 1972.

Wuest's Word Studies. *The Greek New Testament.* Grand Rapids, Michigan: William B. Eerdmans Publishing Co., 1966.

Zodhiates, Spiros. *The Pursuit of Happiness.* Grand Rapids, Michigan: William B. Eerdmans Publishing Co., 1966.